GARDNER'S GUIDE

TV SITCOM WRITING

The Writer's Road Map

Marilyn Webber

GARTH GARDNER COMPANY

GGC publishing

Washington DC, USA · London, UK

Art Director: Nic Banks
Editorial: Chris Edwards
Publisher: Garth Gardner, Ph.D.
Cover Design: Nic Banks

Editorial inquiries concerning this book should be mailed to: The Editor, Garth Gardner Company, 5107 13th Street N.W., Washington DC 20011 or emailed to: info@ggcinc.com.

http://www.gogardner.com

Library of Congress Cataloging-in-Publication Data

Webber, Marilyn.
    Gardner's guide to TV sitcom writing : the writer's road map / Marilyn Webber.
        p. cm.
"Sitcomography & filmography": p.
    ISBN 1-58965-016-6
    1. Television authorship. 2. Television comedies. I. Title: Guide to TV sitcom writing. II. Title: Gardner's guide to television sitcom writing. III. Title.
    PN1992.7.W39 2003
    808.2'25--dc22   2003019234

Printed in Canada

Table of Contents

Acknowledgements

I want to thank Garth and all those at Garth Gardner Company Publishing who have made this series of books possible. I also would like to say thanks to all those talented sitcom writers, producers, directors, and actors who make us laugh week after week, and lighten our lives with their wonderful sense of comedy.

About the Author

Marilyn Webber has worked closely with writers and producers of such hit sitcoms as *Becker*, *Wings*, and *Flying Blind*. She has won awards and had numerous nominations in her ten-year career as a professional writer. She has freelanced for networks such ABC, CBS, USA, and UPN, and for studios such as Universal and Disney. She has analyzed scripts for some of the top names in the business and consulted with respected sitcom writers in order to bring you this quintessential guide to writing sitcoms. Now, it's up to you to take this knowledge and turn your ideas into hit series and/or becoming a star sitcom writer.

Introduction

Do people constantly profess you're funny? Do friends and even more importantly, non-friends, laugh hysterically at your jokes? Ever dream of writing your own TV sitcom or working as a writer on a hit sitcom? Yes, you say to all of the above? Well then, this book is for you!

Whether you're a novice writer or a writer looking for a new medium to stretch your literary muscles, everything you need to know to turn your idea into a saleable TV sitcom pilot or sample spec script for an existing show is right here. *Gardner's Guide to TV Sitcom Writing: The Writer's Road Map* will guide you through various exercises, helping you turn your story ideas into a sitcom pilot script and/or a spec script for an existing series. These two scripts will be your calling card.

This book, however, will not cover the additional qualities that must be considered when developing an animated sitcom, although you can find this information in *Gardner's Guide to Animation Scriptwriting: The Writer's Road Map*.

Writing for sitcoms is hard work. But it's also a blast, and it can be extremely lucrative. The WGA (Writer's Guild of America) minimum for a sitcom script is around $18,000. Not only do you get paid for the initial script, but every time your episode airs past the original run, you get a residual check (which is generally about half of your original pay for the script, and continues to decrease by half until it reaches a WGA set percentage, somewhere between 3–5%). In addition to all this, you also get paid a one-time foreign residuals fee when your episode(s) appears overseas (and it will). All these checks appear like free money because the work has long been done.

Sounds decent, you think. But you're still not sure a writer's life is for you. Well, consider this. A staff sitcom writer also receives a weekly salary based on his/her experience (in addition to the $18,000 for each script he/she writes; generally, a staff writer will get at least two scripts his/her first year on the sitcom). This salary runs around $1,600 per week for a new writer and up to about $3,500 a week for an experienced writer. With a forty-four year work week (plus an 8 week hiatus) you can see how those dollar signs quickly add up!

Thus, with hundreds of sitcoms produced each year, why not try your hand at becoming a freelance sitcom writer? Once you impress the series' producers (which are the top writers of the show) you can end up with a coveted staff job and be on your way to making the big bucks! Each consecutive year, according to WGA rules, you'll advance up the literary ladder. You will move from a staff position to a story editor to co-producer to producer to co-executive producer, and finally to executive producer where you have the greatest control over your work and also a huge paycheck per episode—especially on network TV.

With all the networks and cable channels popping up, comes the need for more and more product. Each network and many of the cable channels develop twenty-two dozen episodes per series; out of this number, four or five scripts per series are assigned to freelance writers. With the hundreds of sitcoms on air today, that's a lot of job potential! All you need is two half-hour sample scripts that prove your talents as a comedy writer, and you're on your way.

Through simple analogy, *Gardner's Guide to TV Sitcom Writing: The Writer's Road Map*, will explain sitcom genres, popular sitcom plots, styles of comedy, the two act structure, sitcom character types and relationships, scene construction, dialogue devices, and sitcom bibles. It also explains the do's and don'ts of writing sitcoms and/or sitcom pilots, and examines what makes an idea saleable (either for story or series). This book will guide you in developing your story and/or sitcom series ideas into dynamic pitches. In addition, this book also discusses dialogue devices, comedy gimmicks, and joke writing, all of which will teach you how to magnify the laughs and multiply the humor in your scripts. You'll also have numerous checklists that will help keep your scripts on course.

Once you've completed two half-hour scripts, this book provides guidance for developing and pitching your TV sitcom pilot and/or existing series episode ideas to executives.

Regardless of your writing goals, *Gardner's Guide to TV Sitcom Writing: The Writer's Road Map*, will zoom you onto the road of sitcom writing in an easy manner. So stop wasting your brilliant jokes at the dinner table and start putting them on paper. By the time you finish Chapter One, you'll be on your way to a thrilling and prosperous career!

Chapter One
Sitcom Tunnels

As you probably already know, the word sitcom is derived from the words "situational comedy," which simply means that a group of characters are put into a certain situation each week and play that situation out. In a one-hour TV series, the genre truly affects the plot. In sitcoms, it's the characters and their relationships that define the genre and its stories. Thus, sitcoms can be classified into four major genres or tunnels based on the relationships of the characters: the family sitcom, the friends sitcom, the workplace sitcom, and the combo with a lead.

1 The Family Sitcom

This sitcom tunnel generally focuses on the characters in one family or two families. The family can be a couple, a couple with children, or an extended family. The audience watches each week to see what happens to the characters and to view issues relevant to their own families. Often, this sitcom tunnel will have a moral or lesson plotted within its structure, especially if its target audience is children. Depending on the time slot, this genre can play to the preteen, teen, parent audience, or all of the above.

Sitcoms such as *Everybody Loves Raymond* and Reba represent extended families in this genre while *Malcolm in the Middle* and *My Wife & Kids* represent couples with kids. *Mad About You* and *I Love Lucy* originally portrayed couples. *Sister, Sister* and *Full House* play to younger audiences as many of the plots focus on kids. *The Simpsons* and *King of the Hill* categorize the animated family sitcom.

2 The Friends Sitcom

This sitcom tunnel focuses on a group of single friends and how their lives intertwine. Most or all of the characters will be unrelated, but their strong bonds of friendship form a surrogate family. Sometimes this tunnel debates various sides of a moral and/or ethical issue, using its characters to present different points of view on the subject. Those sitcoms in this tunnel which relate well to teenagers are most often set in a school environment, but may also include the character's home life as well.

Sitcoms such as *Friends, Will & Grace,* and *Seinfeld* illustrate this tunnel through ensemble casts while *Saved by the Bell* and *South Park* (an animated sitcom) showcase preteen and teen friendships. Both are set in the school arena. *Golden Girls* became a huge hit by cleverly seeking an older target audience that most of television had ignored. Since it also dealt with issues that were relevant to a wider audience, it remained at the top ten of highest rated shows for many years.

3 The Workplace Sitcom

Our third tunnel usually depicts an interesting work environment as it explores the relationships of co-workers, bosses, employees, higher-ups, and wannabe's. While storylines might involve family members and home life, the main plots generally center around the workplace and the main cast will comprise those in the office. This tunnel deals with issues and situations that the viewer might experience in his or her own career, or in trying to balance work and family. *M*A*S*H, Becker,* and *Scrubs* are examples of sitcoms in this tunnel.

4 The Combo With A Lead

This tunnel combines a family or friend genre with the workplace genre, more evenly balancing storylines between the two arenas. It has a star or lead character, whose name generally appears in the title. Almost all the A-stories will spin from this star character, at least in the original pilot year. *Frasier, Drew Carey,* and *Mary Tyler Moore* are examples of The Combo With A Lead tunnel. Dr. Katz, an animated sitcom, also fits into this category.

Tunnel Vision—Styles Of Comedy

The style of comedy will determine what kind of jokes are acceptable and consistent with the sitcom for which you are writing. Basically, comedy can be broken down into three categories: broad or farcical comedy, satirical comedy, or cerebral comedy. Each are not necessarily independent of the others, but are most likely blended together in a series. One of these styles or tones of comedy, however, will likely dominate a series. You must capture the dominant tone of the series in your story ideas and your script. You wouldn't try to write a physical comedy script for *Frasier* or a cerebral comedy script for *Married With Children*.

This doesn't mean that *Frasier* would never incorporate a physical comedy bit in the script. It just means that physical comedy will not dominate the story.

1 Broad or Farcical Comedy

Farce is based on ludicrously improbable events and extremely ridiculous situations. It is absurd in its tone—think *Seinfeld*. Farce/Broad comedy contains a lot of physical comedy which means that it encompasses numerous prat falls and physical mishaps. Here, characters are more likely to be just caricatures and one dimensional, rather than be fully developed characters. *Three's Company* is a great example of a sitcom that derived many of its laughs from the physical comedy of a very talented actor, John Ritter. Since Ritter was so adept at performing physical comedy, this became the dominant comedic style of the series. Farce also contains a bit of the burlesque, which means off-color or blue material humor. Potty humor, sex jokes, and puns abound in this tone of comedy. *Married With Children* is another example of a broad or farcical sitcom.

2 Satirical Comedy

In this style of comedy, the use of ridicule, irony, or sarcasm is used to expose folly or vice. Satire brings ridicule onto something or someone else. It will contain cynical observations, sarcasm, and humorous criticisms. The show's characters often mock, tease, or spoof other characters. The humor can sometimes be irreverent and is generally flippant in tone. *M*A*S*H* is a prime example of a sitcom whose dominate comedic style is satire as is *Will & Grace*.

3 Cerebral Comedy

This type of comedy shoots for the intellect. It is brainy humor and a bit high brow. Characters are witty, clever, and intelligent, and this is depicted in their dialogue, although not always their actions. *Frasier* and the English *Black Adder series* would fall into this style of comedy.

Remember. The above categories are just to make you aware of what comedic tone might dominate a certain series. But most sitcoms will have a mixture of all three comedy styles. Whatever tone dominates or blends, be sure that that's the tone you capture in your sample script.

Okay, let's start developing your sitcom pilot and story ideas. In the exercises below, choose two sitcoms which have been on the air for at least a year and one that is currently "hot"; that is, splashed across magazines and entertainment news shows. You want to write for a sitcom that has good ratings and critical acclaim, one that is respected among the industry. Don't associate yourself with a sitcom that may not return to television the following season, no matter how much you may love it, because then your spec script won't be current. Also pick a sitcom that fits with your own style of humor. Show off your talents and go with what you know!

In addition, pick a series that you're passionate about as you will be watching it over and over. Don't, however, choose the series for which you eventually want to write. For legal reasons, producers usually won't read sample scripts written for their own sitcom, and even if they did, no matter how brilliant and witty your script is, you'll never convince them that you know their characters better than they do.

NOTE: Those who want to write two sample scripts for two different existing sitcoms will follow the "A" exercises. Those creating an original sitcom will develop a pilot for a series and a sample script from an existing sitcom and will follow the "B" exercises. This means you will have a script which illustrates that you can write for someone else's characters and TV world as well as create your own.

Exercise 1A: Record and view six episodes for each of the two sitcoms that you've chosen to write your sample scripts for. That's a total of three hours for each sitcom.

Exercise1B: Record and view six episodes for the one sitcom you've chosen to write your sample script (for a total of three hours).

Chapter Two
The Central Idea

The central idea of a sitcom is the fuel that drives your story. In a sentence or two, it sums up who and what your story is about. In addition, if the sitcom you are writing for incorporates a moral or lesson into its plot lines, then you'll have to develop a moral or lesson around the central idea as well. So, just where do those great ideas come from?

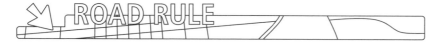

Road Rule #1: A great story idea always derives from a character—especially in sitcoms.

The following ideas were used by writers to build a full story around:

In "The Checkbook," from *Everybody Loves Raymond,* Raymond's immaturity and big mouth get him into trouble yet again and spin the story. After Raymond stupidly scoffs at what's so hard about managing the checkbook, Debra makes Raymond take over the household finances.

In "Leo Unwrapped," from *Will & Grace,* the central idea derives from Will's affection for his best friend, Grace. Will secretly flies Leo home from Africa to surprise Grace on her birthday.

In "Adam's Ribs," from *M*A*S*H,* Hawkeye's obsession for getting barbecue ribs from his favorite restaurant back in the United States weaves the story.

Depending on the sitcom there may be anywhere from one to five storylines weaved within an episode. The first storyline is known as the main plot or the A-story which contains your central idea. The first important subplot is known as the B-story. The next subplot is the C-story, and the next the D-story, and so on. The A-story and B-story will comprise most of your script's pages, although in an ensemble cast series such as *Friends,* the plot lines play out more evenly in regard to how much screen time each story receives. You have just 22 minutes to tell your story (that's half an hour minus the commercials). Thus, you will have to write about 30 scripted pages in film format or 44 pages in tape format because of its unique spacing (we'll discuss format more in a later chapter).

Comedic Catalysts & Complications

You probably already have several story ideas or you wouldn't have bought this book. But if you have difficulty thinking of a storyline, or if you're worried whether or not your story will fit well into the sitcom format, check it against these most popular comedic catalysts and complications. If you mix and match these central idea gimmicks, you'll build more plot tension and more humor.

- The Advice or Favor
- The Bet or Contest
- Break, Lose, or Throw Out
- Controversial/Current/Hot Topics
- The Curse/Threat/Stalker
- The Dead Body
- The Dilemma
- The Discovery/Surprise

- Everyday Stuff
- Examine/Reveal Character Trait
- Famous Firsts
- Holiday Classics
- The Imposter or Mistaken Identity
- The Lie
- Love Stories
- Major Life Events
- The Misunderstanding
- The Mystery
- The Obsession
- Redemption/Righting a Wrong
- The Rescue/Good Samaritan
- Revenge
- The Rivalry
- The Scheme
- The Secret
- Stranded/Trapped
- The Temptation
- The Ticking Clock
- The Trip (exciting locale)
- The Unwanted Gift
- The Visitor
- The Voyeur

1 The Advice or Favor

In this concept, one character gives another character advice which generally proceeds to wreak havoc on the character that follows it. With The Favor concept, one character asks another character to do him/her a big favor which the second character reluctantly agrees to do; chaos ensues.

In "Cyrano De-Beckerac," Becker realizes one of his patient's is dating Reggie, so Becker offers some free advice on how the guy should "court" her.
—*Becker*

In "For Want of a Boot," no favor is too big or too small for Hawkeye who's determined to get a new pair of boots to keep his feet from freezing in the cold Korean winter. But for Zale to get Hawkeye the boots, Hawkeye must get Zale an appointment with the camp dentist, who wants a pass to Tokyo from Henry who wants Houlihan off his back who wants Hawkeye's and the gang to throw a birthday party for Major Burns—complete with a real cake. Radar will get the cake if he can have a date with Nurse Murphy who agrees if she can get a hair dryer. Klinger will give up his hair dryer if he can get a Section 8, but Major Burns refuses to sign the Section 8! Alas, the deal falls through to Hawkeye's dismay.
—*M*A*S*H*

2 The Bet or Contest

Here, two or more characters wager a bet, and the plot and humor spin from this catalyst as each character tries to defeat the other.

In "The Contest," Jerry, Elaine, George, and Kramer see who can become, "Master of his (or her) domain." Need I say more? Not if I want to keep this book G-rated.
—*Seinfeld*

In "No Laughing Matter," Hawkeye wagers that he can go a full day without a wisecrack. Anyone want to take odds on that?
—*M*A*S*H*

3 Break, Lose, or Throw Out

In this popular central idea, a character breaks, loses, or throws out something that is valuable (sentimentally or financially) to another character.

In "The Lucky Suit," Marie accidentally ruins Robert's lucky suit by leaving an iron imprint on the back shoulder. Of course this happens on the biggest day of his life, the day he has an interview with the FBI.
—*Everybody Loves Raymond*

In "Give Him the Chair," Frasier donates Martin's favorite chair to charity, hoping to get rid of the eyesore and convince his dad to enjoy the stylish and fancy new chair he's bought.
—*Frasier*

4 Controversial/Current Trends/Hot Topics

Using this comedic concept, you want to spin your story from a current trend, hot topic, or a controversial topic. If using the controversial topic, you'll want to have different characters present different viewpoints on the issue so that it is fairly presented.

In "Uh Oh," Part 3, Murphy decides to have the baby and not marry, but be a single mom. This sparked a heated debate nationwide about "family values."
—*Murphy Brown*

In the episode below, breast implants were hitting their peak (pun intended) at the time:

In "Big Haas and Little Falsie," Mary Jo inherits money which she must spend on something frivolous, so she considers having breast implants.
—*Designing Women*

5 The Curse/Threat/Stalker

Here, the story spins from a curse or threat made against the character, or someone stalks the character.

In "Someone To Watch Over Me," Frasier is convinced a crazed fan is stalking him so he hires a bodyguard to protect him—a female bodyguard.
—*Frasier*

In "The Slumber Party," the gals chaperone Mary Jo's daughter's slumber party while they anxiously await to see if a voodoo curse put on Suzanne by her maid will come to fruition.
—*Designing Women*

In "The Opera," Elaine's psycho-boyfriend, Crazy Joe, threatens to put the "kibosh" on Jerry.
—*Seinfeld*

6 The Dead Body

It's always fun to mine humor from this catalyst or complication by surprising characters with a dead body, human or animal, especially at the worst possible time.

In "The Kippers & the Corpse," one of the guests dies and Basil assumes it's from the kippers. So begins a game of hide the body so the other guests won't find out.
—*Fawlty Towers*

In "The Seal Who Came To Dinner," Niles hosts a dinner party in an attempt to win the highly coveted Golden Apron Award. He hosts the party at his estranged wife's beach house, but panics when he discovers a horrible odor belonging to a dead seal on the beach.
—*Frasier*

7 The Dilemma

With this concept, a lesson or moral can be explored as the character struggles to make the right decision.

In "Unoriginal Sin," Steve insists that their baby be christened in the Catholic Church, but Miranda isn't religious and isn't sure she wants to christen the baby. She debates on whether to have the christening to make Steve happy, even if it's against her beliefs.
—*Sex & the City*

In "Call Me Irresponsible," Frasier starts dating a woman after he advises her boyfriend to break up with her. But when the boyfriend decides he wants her back, Frasier struggles with the ethical dilemma of assisting the boyfriend and losing the woman, or keeping the two apart so he can keep dating her.
—*Frasier*

8 The Discovery/Surprise

Here, one character discovers something he/she previously didn't know, and is surprised by the revelation.

In "The One Where Old Yeller Dies," Phoebe is traumatized to discover how Old Yeller really ends, realizing that her mother never let her see any unhappy endings.
—*Friends*

In "Leo Unwrapped," Grace is surprised to find her husband home, discovering that Will has flown Leo in from Africa so she could be with him on her birthday.
—*Will & Grace*

9 Everyday Stuff & Stories about Nothing

Everyday stuff spins a lot of sitcom stories because viewers relate to just the simple and basic tasks we perform to get through the day. This concept takes the mundane and makes it funny. The writers of *Seinfeld* were ingenious at writing about everyday or nothing tasks and events, and making us laugh.

In "The Stall," Elaine realizes too late that her stall is out of toilet paper. She becomes upset when a woman won't share toilet paper from the next stall in a public restroom.
—*Seinfeld*

In "What Good Are You?," Debra starts choking, but Raymond doesn't notice. His family's teasing of the incident shames Raymond into being more attentive to such things.
—*Everybody Loves Raymond*

10 Examine/Reveal Character Trait

This is a great way to reveal something more about a character, or examine the traits that viewers already know about the character. Just be sure that if revealing something new about a character, it stays consistent to whom that character is.

In "Turkey Bowl," Jim is one strike away from bowling the perfect game when the power goes out; according to league rules, if he leaves the bowling alley, he forfeits the game. Meanwhile, at home everyone waits for Jim to join them for Thanksgiving dinner.
—*According to Jim*

In "All or Nothing," when Samantha contracts the flu and no one is around to help care for her, she becomes depressed, certain she's going to end up alone.
—*Sex & the City*

11 Famous Firsts

This central idea spins a story about the first time a character experiences a major life event. The first time a character is kissed, learns to drive, leaves home, makes love, fails at something important…you get the idea.

In "The Caste System," Carrie finally summons the courage to tell Big that she loves him. Only his response wasn't what she hoped for—all she gets is an ugly purse.
—*Sex & the City*

In "The Pimple," Kevin is excited to learn an old family friend, Gina, is visiting—until he notices that he's got his first pimple.
—*The Wonder Years*

12 Holiday Classics

Every year around the holidays, you're sure to see a tribute to the most beloved Christmas stories of all time: *It's A Wonderful Life, A Christmas Carol, How the Grinch Stole Christmas, Gift of the Magi, Miracle on 34th Street*. Here, the writer lifts the plot from one of these classics for his/her own episode since these stories are in public domain (which means you can steal them and no one can sue you). Viewers always enjoy a clever twist on these familiar and nostalgic stories.

In "How the Finch Stole Christmas," Finch buys everyone great gifts, but then mistakenly believes they've gotten him nothing so he exchanges their gifts for some mean gag gifts. Fortunately, he has a change of heart, in true Grinch style.
—*Just Shoot Me*

In "A Black Adder's Christmas Carol," a kind and generous Ebeneezer Black Adder is visited by the ghosts of his ancestors who tell him to follow the family tradition.
—*Black Adder*

In a "Miracle on 3rd or 4th Street," Frasier is down in the dumps when Frederick can't spend Christmas with him. But when diners at a café think Frasier is homeless, their kindness brings back his Christmas spirit.
—*Frasier*

13 The Imposter or Mistaken Identity

This catalyst or complication always guarantees laughs. Here, a character either purposely poses as someone else or is mistaken to be someone else by another character, and keeps allowing the mistaken identity to continue.

In "Raybert," a woman in a bar mistakes Robert for Raymond and he plays along since she is a fan of Raymond's.
—*Everybody Loves Raymond*

In "The Limo," when O'Brien, another airplane passenger, doesn't make the plane, George assumes that passenger's identity when he and Jerry see a limo driver waiting for O'Brien.
—*Seinfeld*

14 The Lie

With this catalyst, the character lies, then must keep compounding the lie. The tension builds as the audience waits for the truth to come out. Often this concept combines with the Imposter/Mistaken Identity concept for double the laughs.

In "The Two Mrs. Cranes," an old boyfriend, with whom Daphne broke up with, wants to try again. She then introduces Niles as her husband. Of course, Niles is delighted to oblige, and the lies just get more complicated.
—*Frasier*

In "Tuttle," Hawkeye and Trapper invent an imaginary soldier in order to help out the local orphanage. But the lie snowballs as everyone wants to be Tuttle's friend, and the army wants to give Private Tuttle a medal!
—*M*A*S*H*

15 Love Stories

Loves stories are always popular. They are often told in a matchmaker or fix-up plot, secret admirer plot, lust plot, the pursuer-pursuee plot, and the infamous love-hate plot (remember Sam Malone and Diane Chambers from *Cheers*?). Love plots make great runners or threads (storylines which continue throughout the series, not just one episode).

In "Moon Dance," Daphne teaches Niles to dance so he won't be embarrassed at the upcoming Moon Ball, and then his date cancels on him. When Daphne offers to be his date for the evening, it's heaven on earth for the long suffering Niles who's secretly been in love with Daphne for years.
—*Frasier*

In "Jake's Nuts Roasting on an Open Fire," Jake finally finds the courage to admit his feelings to Dylan by giving her a book of poetry with a special inscription. But it doesn't quite go as planned.
—*Good Morning Miami*

16 Major Life Events

This comedic catalyst spins a story from major life events and life questions such as anniversaries, births, birthdays, first kiss, funerals, having kids, high school reunions, or writing a will…Viewers relate well to this concept because it's something everyone has or will experience in life.

In "Allie's Birth," Raymond attends his first father-daughter dance and reminisces about the day his daughter, Allie, was born.
—*Everybody Loves Raymond*

In "Chuckles Bites the Dust," a beloved clown from the station dies in a bizarre accident and Mary finds Murray's jokes about the death offensive.
—*The Mary Tyler Moore Show*

In "The Will," Hal and Lois have a hard time coming up with something of worth to leave their sons.
—*Malcolm in the Middle*

17 The Misunderstanding

This catalyst or complication is great to mine humor as well. A misunderstanding snowballs throughout the story until finally the misunderstanding is cleared up.

In "An Affair To Forget," Frasier believes Maris is having an affair with her fencing instructor. This leads to one of the most hysterical duels ever choreographed and written as Niles takes on the fencing

instructor to defend his wife's honor.
—*Frasier*

In "The Puffy Shirt," Kramer dates a woman who speaks so softly, no one but Kramer understands what she's saying. This leads to Jerry politely answering "yes" to a question she asks, "Will Jerry wear one of her designer shirts when he appears on The Today Show?" Of course, when Jerry discovers the misunderstanding, he reluctantly wears the puffy-pirate shirt on national TV, only to be totally humiliated.
—*Seinfeld*

18 The Mystery

This is always a fun catalyst because it can add variety to a series that's been on a long time, by taking its characters on a mystery ride.

In "The Usual Suspects," when Becker's office is vandalized, he finds that there are a lot of people who have a plausible motive.
—*Becker*

In "Retirement Is Murder," Martin attempts to solve an old case, "The Weeping Lotus" murder, which involves a prostitute, a cop, and a monkey. Don't ask.
—*Frasier*

19 The Obsession

This concept spins a character's obsession with someone or something. The character grows more obsessed throughout the story, building the tension until finally disaster strikes.

In "The Focus Group," after eleven out of twelve members announce that The Frasier Crane Show is perfect, Frasier obsesses to find out why the twelfth man does not. In the process, he inadvertently destroys the man's life.
—*Frasier*

In "He heard, She Heard," Michael is obsessed with catching his teenage daughter, Claire, and her friends in a lie about going to a party she's forbidden to attend. He'll stop at nothing to prove he's right, but will Claire outsmart him?
—*My Wife & Kids*

20 Redemption

Using this catalyst or complication, you can reveal something from a character's past or present as the character attempts to right a wrong.

In "Liar, Liar," Frasier seeks out a man, now in prison, that was punished in prep school for something Frasier and Niles did, hoping to ease his guilt that the Cranes were not responsible for this man's life of crime.
—*Frasier*

In "The Busboy," George inadvertently gets a busboy fired and then tries to make amends.
—*Seinfeld*

21 The Rescue/Good Samaritan

Here, one character rescues another character from a difficult situation, or a character simply performs a good deed in an attempt to help a stranger.

In "Good Samaritan," Jerry tries to be a good Samaritan by tracking down a hit-and-run driver, but then decides he wants to date her instead.
—*Seinfeld*

In "Gourmet Night," a chef gets plastered the night of a very special dinner and Basil must save the day by delivering a delicious meal to the cream of English society.
—*Fawlty Towers*

22 Revenge

This is always a popular idea as one character makes an attempt to get back at another character. Remember, just be consistent with the character's personality.

In "Past & Presents," Will's worst enemy is hired at the firm and Will seeks revenge by messing up the contract and making his childhood classmate look like an idiot.
—*Will & Grace*

In "Grand Slam, Thank You, Ma'am," Suzanne vows to get even when her baseball star ex-husband reveals all in his racy autobiography.
—*Designing Women*

23 The Rivalry

This central idea builds the story from an intense rivalry between two characters. This one works well with guest stars.

In "A Chorus Lie," Jack adamantly strives to get rid of a tough rival in hopes of getting the last spot on the Manhattan Gay Men's Chorus. He talks Grace into proving the rival's really a straight man and thus, ineligible to compete. (Guest star Matt Damon played the rival competitor.)
—*Will & Grace*

In "Gift Horse," Frasier and Niles compete to see who will get their father the best birthday present. As usual, their rivalry spins out of control.
—*Frasier*

24 The Scheme

This catalyst can be truckloads of fun as one character schemes to get something he/she desires, but of course, the scheme always backfires.

In "Bananas, Crackers, and Nuts," Hawkeye pretends to crack up in order to get a pass for Tokyo for some much needed rest. But the scheme backfires when Frank calls in a psychiatrist.
—*M*A*S*H*

In "The Benadryl Brownie," hives break out on Deborah's face and she refuses medicine to clear it up because she is a Christian Scientist, much to Richard's dismay. So Larry and Richard concoct a plan to bake a batch of Benadryl brownies.
—*Curb Your Enthusiasm*

25 The Secret

Here, one or more characters try to keep a secret from the other characters. The tension mounts until the end when the secret is revealed.

In "A Vote for Debra," Debra runs for school president and Ray fears he won't be able to take care of the twins by himself during all the school meetings, so he secretly votes against her.
—*Everybody Loves Raymond*

In "The One With All The Resolutions," Rachel makes a resolution to stop gossiping, but then discovers the whooper of all secrets, and struggles to keep it.
—*Friends*

26 Stranded/Trapped

Having characters trapped or stranded somewhere together can be a great way to reveal more of the characters and their relationships as well as provide lots of humor.

In "The Stranded," Jerry and Elaine are trapped at a bad party after George abandons them there.
—*Seinfeld*

In "Boyz in the Woods," Philip takes Will and Carlton on a camping trip that soon turns to disaster as snow traps the unhappy group.
—*The Fresh Prince of Bel Air*

27 The Temptation

Here, a character is tempted by something that pulls him/her into the plot and gets them into trouble.

In "Diary of a Mad Teen," Jay stumbles on to Claire's diary and can't resist reading it. She is panicked to learn her daughter is thinking about going to the "next step" with her boyfriend.
–*My Wife & Kids*

In "The Juicer," Rudy is tempted by the new, shiny juicer in the kitchen that her dad has ordered her not to play with, which of course makes the object more desirable.
—*The Cosby Show*

28 The Ticking Clock

This plot device is used to heighten the dramatic and comedic tension within the story by serving up an obstacle to the character(s) which they must overcome by a specific time.

In "Club Soda & Salt," after Larry fires the chef, his investors are furious so Larry must find a new chef before opening night of his restaurant.
—*Curb Your Enthusiasm*

In "The Parking Garage," George, Kramer, Elaine, and Jerry search for Kramer's car in the parking lot of the mall after he forgets where he parked as George grows more frustrated: he must be back in the city by 6:30 p.m. for his parent's anniversary dinner and a Broadway show.
—*Seinfeld*

29 The Trip

This can be an entertaining way to get your characters out of their usual surroundings, and even send them to an exciting locale.

In "Travels With Martin," the Cranes and Daphne hit the road in a Winnebago to see Mount Rushmore, but a wrong turn lands them in Canada, and nearly in jail.
—*Frasier*

In "Road Trip," Jay organizes an educational road trip for the family to Paul Revere's house. But Michael is dreading every mile because for both Jay and Claire it's "their time of the month" and that spells trouble!
—*My Wife & Kids*

30 The Unwanted Gift

This concept centers around one character receiving a gift from a loved one or friend that he or she absolutely hates, but doesn't know how to get rid of without hurting the giver's feelings.

In "The Nanny," Larry buys the last dozen sponge cakes for his friend's birthday, but Jeff's wife goes ballistic when Larry delivers them to the house because Jeff needs to lose weight.
—*Curb Your Enthusiasm*

In "Marie's Sculpture," Marie proudly gives Ray and Debra a sculpture she's made in her sculpture class, not realizing that to everyone else, the sculpture looks like a vagina.
—*Everybody Loves Raymond*

31 The Visitor

Creating a new character for an existing series can be fun, especially if you make sure the character's personality or actions upsets the status quo.

In "A Little Romance," Ken, Michael's brother, comes to visit, bringing his latest girlfriend. While Junior ogles the hot babe, Michael's envious of his brother's hot, sex life, feeling his own sex life has become a little dull.
–*My Wife & Kids*

In "Divided We Stand," a psychiatrist arrives to judge whether or not the doctors and nurses in the unit should remain together or be split up because of personality differences.
—*M*A*S*H*

32 The Voyeur

Using this central concept, one character becomes a voyeur, fascinated by one of his/her neighbors.

In "Here's Looking At You," a bored Martin takes up spying on his neighbors via telescope, and then starts dating one of the women he's been watching.
—*Frasier*

In "The Tree House," Kevin and his dad build a tree house in the backyard, only to realize they have a great view of an attractive neighbor planting her tomatoes.
—*The Wonder Years*

From these catalysts and complications, the writers of the examples above spun their central ideas into springboards, which we will examine in the next chapter. As you choose your own central ideas in the exercises below, remember that whatever you think of first, will probably be what everyone else thinks of, too. Brainstorm for fresh ways to use these comedic catalysts and complications, discarding your first five ideas. Most likely, the sixth or seventh idea will really be a clever and fresh twist to these popular story concepts.

Exercise 2: From the previously recorded sitcom episodes from exercise one, list the central ideas of each plot line, making note of any of these catalysts or complications used in the episodes.

NOTE: DO NOT SKIP exercises. You must know the existing series from which you plan to develop your script(s) inside and out. The more work you do in the beginning, the easier and more successful your final drafts will be.

Exercise 3: Choose six central ideas (use the comedic catalysts and complications if you like) to build a story for your first script, regardless of whether you are writing for an existing series or creating an original pilot.

Chapter Three
Springboards

A springboard includes the central idea from which the A-story "springs," but also adds the second plot twist or hook in the story. Thus, the springboard sums up the beginning, middle, and end of the A-story. In sitcoms, a springboard may also be called the premise. Regardless, the springboard or premise is your 3–6 sentence pitch to the executive and/or producer, explaining what and who your main plot is about.

In the springboard, you also want to capture the tone of the sitcom. If you develop a springboard for a physical comedy sitcom, your springboard should reflect physical comedy; if you develop a springboard for a cerebral wit sitcom, your springboard should reflect intellectual humor.

Let's say you're writing a sample episode for *Everybody Loves Raymond* with Raymond as your lead character. You would probably create ideas which would "spring" from something stupid that Ray does and then has to get himself out of. If writing for *Frasier*, the story would most likely center around Frasier trying to impress someone or Frasier and Niles competing. If writing an episode for *Sabrina, The Teenage Witch*, your story would probably spring from

Sabrina or another witch/warlock's magic reeking havoc until Sabrina finds a way to solve the problem.

Let's look at some possible springboards for some episodes that aired:

In "Raybert," a woman in a bar mistakes Robert for Raymond and he plays along since she is a fan of Raymond's (central idea). Only when she shows up at Ray's and tells Debra, whom she thought was dead, that she and Ray are dating, all heck breaks lose (plot twist).
—*Everybody Loves Raymond*

In "The Usual Suspects," when Becker's office is vandalized, he finds that there are a lot of people who have a plausible motive (central idea). It turns out that Linda is the guilty one; she was throwing a party and things got out of hand. She tries to keep the secret by dating the clueless cop assigned to the case (twist).
—*Becker*

In "The Limo," O'Brien, another passenger on George's plane, doesn't make the flight and George assumes his identity when he and Jerry see a limo driver waiting for O'Brien (central idea). Too late, they discover that George has assumed the identity of a Neo-Nazi leader who's on his way to deliver a hate rallying speech (plot twist).
—*Seinfeld*

In "Dial M For Martin," Daphne goes to work elsewhere as Martin has completely recovered and no longer needs her as a physical therapist (central idea). When Martin starts having "accidents" at Nile's place, Martin begins to fear that his son is unconsciously trying to injure him so that Daphne will come back to work and live with them (plot twist).
—*Frasier*

In "Chuckles Bites the Dust," a beloved clown from the station dies in a bizarre accident and Mary finds Murray's jokes about the death offensive (central idea). She feels they shouldn't be laughing, but when they all attend Chuckle's funeral, it's Mary who can't stop laughing (plot twist).
—*The Mary Tyler Moore Show*

Story Road Flags

To help develop your central idea into a saleable springboard or premise, you must answer as succinctly and as excitingly, these story flags which will help formulate your plot:

1 Who is the A-story about?

2 What is the predicament and will it spin lots of humor?

3 What is the surprise twist or complication that shoots the story in a new direction?

4 What does the character want?

5 What or who provides an obstacle to the character's goal?

Let's see how these story flags play out in the examples below:

NOTE: The examples below are not the original springboards, but a sample of plausible springboards for these episodes.

In "The Canister," Debra feels Marie is calling her a liar and a thief when she doesn't accept her word that she has returned a treasured family canister, so Debra demands an apology. Marie apologizes, never meaning to have hurt Debra's feelings. Only, after Marie leaves, Debra discovers she really does have the canister. Panicked, Debra convinces Ray and Robert that it's in all their best interests to sneak the canister back into Marie's house, or they'll never hear the end of it! Will they succeed or be forever doomed to Marie's, "I'm always right, remember the canister?"
—*Everybody Loves Raymond*

Does the springboard above pass all our story flags? Let's break it down:

Flag 1: Debra

Flag 2: Debra insists she doesn't have the canister Marie loaned her, making such a scene until Marie apologizes, only to learn soon after that she does indeed still have the canister. The competition between these two women insures this predicament will provided tons of humor.

Flag 3: When the canister keeps reappearing like a dead body, Debra and Ray scheme to sneak the canister back into Marie's house.

Flag 4: At first, Debra wants Marie to admit to being wrong. Once, Debra realizes Marie's right, Debra wants to successfully sneak the canister back into Marie's house so Marie will never know.

Flag 5: Marie is the opposition, although she is inadvertently keeping Debra from succeeding by popping in and out of the room as they try to hide the canister.

As you can see, this springboard covers all the story road flags. The writer began with a character trait and the discovery catalyst to form their central idea, then complicated it by adding the scheme plot.

Let's look at an example from the friends genre, using the series, *Friends*:

In "The One Where Joey Loses His Insurance," Joey discovers his SAG insurance has lapsed and immediately pursues an acting job to regain qualification for benefits. But in true Joey style, he injures himself while trying to get back into shape. He's in so much pain from the hernia, that it ruins all his auditions; that is, until he gets an audition to play a dying father. The question is, can Joey survive long enough to finish the job when the child actor keeps blowing the scene?
—*Friends*

Flag 1: Joey

Flag 2: Joey's Screen Actor Guild (SAG) insurance has lapsed.

Flag 3: To get a job so he can get his SAG insurance back before something bad happens to him. Unfortunately, he injures himself as he tries to get back into shape for auditions.

Flag 4: Joey injures himself, but can't go to the doctor because he has no insurance, so he keeps auditioning even though he's in pain and can hardly move. There's obviously plenty of humor to mine from this complication.

Flag 5: His injury and then his kid co-star hinder his efforts to achieving his goal.

The central idea: Joey gets a letter stating his SAG insurance has lapsed, and must get an acting job immediately to get it back (the discovery catalyst). The writer then rounded it into a full storyline: a beginning (Joey's insurance lapses and he must get an acting job) a middle (Joey injures himself and the injury keeps ruining his auditions and his goal of getting insurance) and an end (Joey gets hired to play a dying father saying goodbye to his ten-year old son).

In a *Fawlty Towers* episode "Basil the Rat," Basil Fawlty discovers his busboy Manuel's pet rat and demands that Manuel get rid of the "hamster" before the hotel inspector shows up. But Manuel hides his pet instead. When the rat is discovered missing, the other servants and Basil search frantically for it, trying to keep the hotel inspector from discovering there's a rat in the hotel.

Flag 1: Manuel and his pet "hamster" which is really a rat.

Flag 2: The hotel inspector is coming and Manuel must get rid of his beloved pet rat, but decides to hide it instead.

Flag 3: The rat escapes its cage and is on the loose in the hotel.

Flag 4: Manuel wants to keep his pet (Basil wants to get a good rating from the hotel inspector). Notice how these two goals are in direct conflict, which makes for great dramatic tension as the viewer waits for the two goals to collide.

Flag 5: The rat and the hotel inspector threaten both Manuel and Basil's goals.

Once again, all the story road flags are answered, revealing the beginning, middle, and end of the story.

Series Road Flags

If you are creating your own sitcom series as well, you'll need to answer these following series flags:

1 Who are the characters?

2 What is the situation and is there enough comedy in the situation of the series setup to fuel years of episodes?

3 What is the marketability or hook of your story? That is, what makes the network drooling to buy it and what makes the series exciting to viewers?

The Hook

Executives want to hear that something special. Giving your story a hook just means you're taking an idea and spinning it in a unique way to make your story idea high-concept. High-concept means that you can pitch your series in one or two sentences and network executives can immediately see dollar signs. For example, "A Teen *Bewitched*." Right away, executives can see the marketability, and did, with *Sabrina the Teenage Witch*. Not to mention, using a marquee character that already has recognition via comic books with its target audience (preteen and teenage girls).

"*American Graffiti* for the generation weaned on Frampton, *The Brady Bunch*, 8-track tapes, and all manner of fashion disasters. Set in small-town Wisconsin in 1976, …a likable group of aimless teens look for a good time anywhere, whether attending a Todd Rundgren concert or sneaking beers in a friend's basement." *(That 70's Show)*

*Excerpt from TV Guide, Fall Preview Issue 1998

Frasier was built around a character that viewers were already familiar with, surrounding the title character with a wonderful cast of interesting and neurotic characters. The hook was a sitcom about a successful radio psychiatrist who was crazier than his callers and whose life was a mess.

Seinfeld took a star comedian and created a show with four quirky and eccentric characters. The hook here was that every week the episode would be about nothing, just the minutia of everyday obsessions and lives of these characters.

NOTE: Originally, the series did not include the Elaine character, but after testing low with a market audience, they added the female character of Elaine, and a hit series was born. This was a bit of a risk, but it paid off BIG TIME!

In *3rd Rock From the Sun*, the hook is a family sitcom where none of the characters are related. Instead, they are members of an alien military squadron pretending to be a family with one male alien even posing as a female human.

The pitch for this series might have gone something like this:

A group of aliens are sent to Earth on a mission to study the human race. No one can know their secret, so they pose as a human family; one alien ordered to be the kid while another male alien must masquerade as a female human. This is a true fish out of water story, or should I say, alien out of his world. Can this crazy group of extraterrestrials successfully complete their mission by posing as a caring family when they can barely tolerate each other?

Does this pitch use all the series road flags? Let's examine:

Flag 1: A group of extraterrestrials trying to study the human race.

Flag 2: Aliens trying to pose as humans and trying to keep their secret each week.

Flag 3: There's too much fun and laughs to be had from this setup, that's what makes it so marketable. Since they pose as a family, they will be dealing with family issues that make it relatable to viewers.

Try these exercises.

Exercise 4A: Take your central ideas, and combine each of them with a story complication or twist to create six fresh springboards for your first sample script. Be sure your springboards answer all the story road flags. Capture the comedic tone of the series in each premise.

Exercise 4B: For those creating an original series, complete exercise 4A, then create a sitcom springboard using all three series road flags to develop your pilot pitch. Be sure your series has a saleable hook and is relatable.

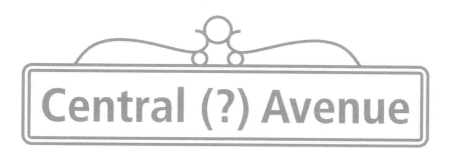

Central (?) Avenue

Chapter Four
Dead End Ahead—The Central Question

The central question of your story is the focus of a plot, and the question which is answered in the course of an episode, a story arc (over several episodes), or a series. It is answered in the climax (the big clash or confrontation). The viewer must not know the answer to the central question until the end of the episode, story arc, and/or series. On your Writer's Road Map, this question is labeled "Central (?) Avenue."

Road Rule #2: Before you construct your plot, know where your road ends. Knowing the ending of your story will keep you from writing scenes which wander aimlessly in your script, only to be discarded in the rewrite.

In your script, the Central (?) Avenue of the A-story will be answered in the climax of Act Two. The number of central questions you have per episode depends on how many plot lines you have, but each subplot must have its own central question as well. Whether it is answered in the episode or throughout the series depends on if the plot is a runner or thread plot (plots that continue over several episodes).

In "The Canister," episode of *Everybody Loves Raymond* the central question is: "Will Marie find out she was right—Debra really did still have the canister?!"

In the *Friends* episode "The One Where Joey Loses Insurance," the central question of the A-story is, "Will Joey get an acting job so his insurance will be reinstated?" The B-story central question is "Will Ross succeed as a lecturer and get the professor appointment at NYU?" The C-story central question is, "Will Phoebe die at the end of the episode as the psychic predicted?" The D-story is, "Will Rachel find out she's still married to Ross?" One of the episodic or continuing storylines of the series is: "Will Ross and Rachel finally get together as a couple?" The central questions to the A, B, C, and D plots are answered in the climax of the episode while the E-story (Will Rachel and Ross finally get together?) continues to be a running plot in the series.

In the "Get Out" episode of *My Wife & Kids*, the central question is, "Will Michael be able to get his family dressed and to his cousin's wedding on time?"

Continuing Central Question

Often, there is a continuing central question that weaves throughout a sitcom and runs the length of the series, or at least for several seasons. If the sitcom for which you are writing has a continuing central question, you could use it to build one of your plots around. In sitcoms, most of the continuing central questions spin from love plots. For example:

Frasier: "Will Niles and Daphne finally get together?"

Sex & the City: "Will the girls find true love?"

Friends: "Will Ross and Rachel get together?"

The continuing central question, however, doesn't always have to be about romance. For example:

M*A*S*H: "Will the characters survive the Korean War and get to go home?"

If you are creating an original pilot, you might want to add a continuing central question for your series because it's a fabulous way to keep viewers tuning in week after week.

Exercise 5: Before you develop your own central question avenues for each plot (A-E stories, if applicable) identify those from the stories in the six or twelve episodes you watched for exercise one. Are there any continuing series questions? You might want to incorporate it as one of your subplots.

Exercise 6: Write the central question for the A-story (main plot) and for any other subplots you're creating for your first script.

Chapter Five
Sitcom Characters

The Driver(s)

Sitcoms work with ensemble casts, generally favoring four to seven main characters from which they spin their stories. These are the characters that are usually depicted in the opening credits. Even though they work with an ensemble cast, some sitcoms also have a main character or driver as the lead of the episode/series, and the one who will drive most of the A-stories. Regardless, if the series has a lead, most sitcoms encompass four to seven characters in the main cast.

1 The 4-Cast Sitcom

Here, four main characters form the cast, but usually one takes the lead and carries the A-story plot each week. *Seinfeld, Sex & the City,* and *Will & Grace* all have lead drivers. Every A-story will go to Jerry Seinfeld, Carrie Bradshaw, Will Truman, and/or Grace Adler-Markus. The A-story plot will consume most of the story's screen time while the subplots will be divided among the other three characters, either equally or with a strong B-story plot. These series generally have one to three plots running through them and are well suited to the friends genre.

2 The 5-Cast Sitcom

This cast supports five main characters from which to spin the A-D stories. Sitcoms such as *Everybody Loves Raymond, My Wife & Kids,* and *Frasier* fall into this category. Family sitcoms fit well here because it allows for the parents and three kids. The A-story most likely will fall to the parents, like Ray and Debra in *Everybody Loves Raymond,* or Michael and Jay in *My Wife & Kids* who are the lead characters, or the title character, like in *Frasier.* Subplots will generate from the children or other family members/coworkers, such as Niles, Roz, Daphne, and Martin in *Frasier.*

3 The 6-8 Cast Sitcom

This type of cast of characters allows you greater creative range, because often there are many characters from which to derive the plots. The series is told every week from numerous viewpoints, or the viewpoint of a different character than the week before unless the cast does have a lead character. This cast type generally has more subplots than the four or five cast sitcoms. Here, the A-story can be dominated by the lead character, like Becker (*Becker*) or Drew (*The Drew Carey Show*) and supported by a sublot, or the A-story and subplots can be more evenly divided among the ensemble cast, as in *Friends* and *That 70's Show*. The A-story will always dominate, but it may not take up most of the half hour. Instead, the A-story can be more evenly divided among the subplots. The friend and work tunnels fit well with this type of cast.

Popular Sitcom Character Types

In sitcoms, there are numerous popular character types, but all must be relatable to the viewer. Thus, if you are creating your own series:

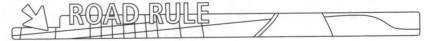

Road Rule #3: Give the viewer characters to care about, and ones we can laugh and cry with along the ride.

Your characters must have the same needs, desires, dreams, obsessions, and problems that the viewer might have. This is what makes a viewer identify with the driver of the episode and/or series. To help make characters relatable, the creators start by choosing several of these popular sitcom character types to cast their series:

- Bossy/Pushy
- Buffoon/Dumb/Idiot
- Extraterrestrials
- Father Doesn't Know Best
- Girl/Guy-Next Door

- Intellectual Snob/Braggart
- Klutz
- Lovable Loser
- Lovable Lunatic
- Nerd
- Obsessive A-type Career Woman/Man
- Prima Donna
- Quirky/Eccentric
- Rebel
- Sarcastic Wisecracker
- Sassy, Man-Crazy Woman
- Sensible Moms
- Spirited Spirits
- Trouble-Maker
- Wisecracking Kid

1 Bossy/Pushy

This character bosses the other characters in the show around; he/she is the "alpha dog" of the show. While he/she is pushy, it generally comes from his/her love or concern for the other characters in the cast.

Marie Barone—*Everybody Loves Raymond*

Hyacinth Bucket—*Keeping Up Appearances*

Lois Wilkerson—*Malcolm in the Middle*

2 Dumb/Idiot/Buffoon

This character is, well, just plain stupid. He/she can vary in his/her degree of stupidity, but should stay consistent with that level of ignorance. The viewer can laugh at this character, but in an endearing way, of course. He/she generally has a heart of gold, but just has a few dots missing on his/her dominoes.

Oswald Lee Harvey—*The Drew Carey Show*

Joey Tribbianni—*Friends*

Linda—*Becker*

3 Extraterrestrials

These characters are out of this world, and so can take on unique powers as part of their character traits. Because of this, and because of the "fish-out-of-water" setup, they are a great place from which to mine humor.

High Commander Dick Solomon, Security Officer Sally Solomon, Communicator Harry Solomon, and Information Officer Tommy Solomon –*3rd Rock from the Sun*

Alf—*Alf*

4 Father Doesn't Know Best

Dads have change since Jim Anderson (Father Knows Best). Often, dads are portrayed as not getting it right most of the time. Although they mean well, they just don't fully understand how to best play the parenting game. This character is a good dad at heart, but he makes a lot of mistakes which are usually corrected by the sensible mom.

Hal Wilkerson—*Malcolm in the Middle*

Raymond Barone—*Everybody Loves Raymond*

Tim Taylor—*Home Improvement*

5 Girl/Guy-Next Door

This is one of the most popular character types because viewers relate to this character. He/she is the girl or boy next door with the usual everyday life problems. At least one of your characters on the series will probably fall into this category.

Martin Crane—*Frasier*

Maya Gallo—*Just Shoot Me*

Elaine Benes—*Seinfeld*

6 Intellectual Snob

This character carries an air of superiority over the rest of the cast due to his/her intellect. Therefore, this character is often a braggart as well. This character, however, may not have a lot of common sense and/or social skills. His/her intellect and/or bragging often get this character into trouble.

Frasier Crane—*Frasier*

Charles Winchester—*M*A*S*H*

Niles Crane—*Frasier*

7 Klutz

This character brings a lot of physical comedy to the series by their klutzy nature.

Kramer—*Seinfeld*

Jack Tripper—*Three's Company*

8 Lovable Loser

This character gets slammed from all directions, always ending up on the bottom of the pile—fate just appears to be against him/her. Thus, the character often has low self-esteem and is self-deprecating. They are acutely aware of their limitations, whether real or self-imposed. The underdog who rarely triumphs, this character immediately wins the viewer's sympathy.

Homer Simpson—*The Simpsons*

George Castanza—*Seinfeld*

Robert Barone—*Everybody Loves Raymond*

9 Lovable Lunatic

This character is wacky, kooky, and way out there! This character just has an extremely original POV about the world around him/her and also marches to his/her own drummer.

Klinger—*M*A*S*H*

Kramer—*Seinfeld*

Major Gowen—*Fawlty Towers*

10 Nerd

This character is geeky and just a bit out of step with the cool crowd.

This type is always popular with viewers because he/she is generally socially inept and awkward when it comes to affairs of the heart.

Ross—*Friends*

Niles—*Frasier*

Fez—*That 70's Show*

11 Obsessive A-type

This character has some degree of OCB (Obsessive-Compulsive Disorder) which is a great place to derive humor. They are often anal-retentive and ambitious. Sometimes they can be relentless in their pursuit of something which can fuel numerous and funny plot lines. Often, this character is a leader and an over achiever.

Will Truman—*Will & Grace*

Monica Gellar Chandler—*Friends*

Miranda Hobbs—*Sex & the City*

12 Prima Donna

This character feels a sense of entitlement and is packed full of confidence. Vain, selfish, obnoxious, and narcissistic, this character can drive the other characters in the story completely nuts at times.

Jack—*Will & Grace*

Suzanne Sugarbaker—*Designing Women*

Karen Walker—*Will & Grace*

13 Quirky/Eccentric

This character is always a great character to have because there's so much humor that just flows naturally from his/her traits. He/she is sometimes clueless (but not dumb) because of the way his/her mind works, which is extremely different from the rest of the characters.

This character really marches to his/her own drummer, sees the world in a very unique way, and sometimes adopts new age philosophy.

Phoebe Buffay—*Friends*

Daddy—*Keeping Up Appearance*s

14 The Rebel

This character doesn't always fit into society's norms, he/she is an outcast; anti-establishment. This can be a good trait, or it can work against the character. This character doesn't look for approval either, but just acts on her/his own instincts, and remains true to the convictions that define him/her. This character lives in the moment. Sometimes, he/she is the bad boy or girl of the series.

Hyde—*That 70's Show*

Francis—*Malcolm in the Middle*

Fonzie—*Happy Days*

15 Sarcastic Wisecracker

This character is witty and clever. He/she loves to verbally spar with the other characters, getting in a witty jab as often as possible.

Hawkeye Pierce—*M*A*S*H*

Jerry Seinfeld—*Seinfeld*

Frank Barrone—*Everybody Loves Raymond*

16 Sassy, Man-Crazed Female

This is a favorite stock character for sitcoms as it is easy to create off-color jokes for this character.

Nina Van Horn—*Just Shoot Me*

Samantha Jones—*Sex & the City*

Rose—*Keeping Up Appearance*s

17 Sensible Moms

Yes, mother knows best with this character type. This character is a down-to-earth nurturer who is often getting her husband and sometimes her kids out of the mess they've gotten themselves into.

Debra Barone—*Everybody Loves Raymond*

Janet (Jay) Kyle—*My Wife & Kids*

Marge Simpson—*The Simpsons*

18 Spirited Spirits

This character is fun to write for because they have special powers which can wreak havoc on other characters and the plots. These characters are endearing because they are outsiders who try so very hard to fit in.

Sabrina Spellman—*Sabrina, the Teenage Witch*

Jeannie—*I Dream of Jeannie*

Samantha Stevens—*Bewitched*

19 Trouble-Maker/Schemer

This character is always up to no good, scheming and playing with the other character's lives. This character just can't help him/herself - this character is just plain ornery.

Dennis Finch—*Just Shoot Me*

Bart Simpson—*The Simpsons*

Randy Taylor—*Home Improvement*

20 Wisecracking Kid

The precocious, smart-aleck kid is a stock character for the family genre.

Darlene Connors—*Roseanne*

Kyra Hart—*Reba*

Bart Simpson—*The Simpsons*

As you can see, you can take one dominate trait, mix it with another, and create a popular sitcom character. These popular characters types are just a helpful start, you'll want to paint the character yourself, updating the character and making him/her fresh and interesting.

Pedestrians or Passengers

These are the characters who "support" the lead character(s), either weekly as a series regular, or sporadically as a recurring character (occasionally throughout the series) or guest character (appearing only once). These characters illuminate the lead character's personality and/or advance the plot. They serve to bounce off dialogue off the main character(s) and are characters from which to derive humor, conflict, and information. Supporting characters can be fun to write because they are often more quirky than your main driver.

In *Seinfeld,* Seinfeld is the lead driver of the series while George, Elaine, Kramer, and occasionally, Newman, Mr. And Mrs. Castanza, Mr. And Mrs. Seinfeld form the supporting cast.

In *Everybody Loves Raymond,* Ray and Debra are most often the drivers of the plots while the supporting cast includes Robert, Marie, Frank, Ray's buddies, Robert's occasional girlfriends, and the kids (Allie, Michael, and Jeffrey).

In *Friends,* the cast is truly an ensemble, where each of the six characters can be the lead character in an episode, the driver of the plot one week and a supporting character the plot the following week. Their boyfriend or girlfriends, siblings, and parents form other supporting cast for the series.

Here are a few exercises to try.

Exercise 7: From the previous one or two series you recorded, list the main cast (those shown in the opening credits). This is the cast you must use in your sample script(s). In addition, if creating your own

series, list your main cast of characters. (Don't describe them yet, we'll get to that in the next chapter. For now, just list the character type.)

Exercise 8: List the supporting characters from the six or twelve episodes you watched. These are the characters you will need to use in your sample script as well if they appear in the main credits. In addition, if creating your own pilot, also list the supporting characters you'll need; those who will be seen in the main credits or will be seen as a reoccurring character throughout the series.

Chapter Six
Character Development

Now that you have a basic idea of popular sitcom character types, let's start developing these characters into more three-dimensional personalities. Writing for characters on television is unique because you have hours and hours of time to develop and layer characters, revealing bits of his/her personality over many episodes and hopefully, over many years. Thus, a viewer gets to really know the characters and become attached to them. It's important to note, however, that sitcom characters don't grow and change in major ways. They keep their same flaws and foibles week after week, remaining as comfortable and familiar to the viewer as an old shoe. The audience tunes in to see what kind of mess the character creates and how he/she is going to squirm out of that predicament. It really wouldn't be funny if the characters matured and outgrew their weaknesses, because then what would be the fun in watching?

Identification Please

Never, ever get into the car with a stranger. If you don't know the driver of your story, you can't write him/her convincingly and consistently.

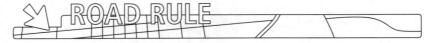

Road Rule #4: Know your characters and how they will react with one another! Stay consistent to the sitcom world and characters you create or attempt to write for in an existing series.

This is paramount to impressing producers. When writing for an existing show, you've got to know who the characters are so you can have them react consistently in the story you are creating. When creating your own series, you've got to know who your characters are so they will be consistent within your own pilot script. How do you do this? By creating a character dipstick and a compass for the characters to follow.

Character Dipsticks

A dipstick consists of everything you create or learn about the character for which you are writing. Dipsticks measure the fundamental characteristics of each character:

- Age
- Environment
- Time Period
- Cultural Background
- Relationships
- Super or Magical Powers (if applicable)

1 **His/Her Approximate Age:** How old is the character?

2 **Environment:** Where does he/she live? Most likely, on planet earth and in the US, but what part of the region?

3 **Time Period:** Is the show contemporary like *My Wife & Kids*? Most likely yes, but it doesn't have to be. It could be a period piece like *M*A*S*H* or a futuristic sitcom like Futurama.

4 **Cultural Background:** Of what nationality or ethnic background do the characters derive? Are they Hispanic *(The George Lopez Show)*

African American (*The Bernie Mac Show*) British *(Fawlty Towers)*...

5 **Relationships:** What is the driver's relationship to the other characters in the story?

The viewer learns about a character by how he/she relates to the other characters around him/her. Thus, you must know how characters relate to each other. Who are his/her friends? Enemies? Parents? Siblings? Classmates? Colleagues? Learn or create their back story (history with one another) to know how your characters will act and react with each other in a scene. For example, are the characters childhood sweethearts or college roommates who haven't seen each other in a decade? How does a character relate to his/her family? This will speak volumes about that character.

In addition, does one character have a kind of shorthand with his wife/husband or best friend like Will Truman and Grace Adler on *Will & Grace*? If one character can finish the other character's sentences or know what that character is thinking by his/her look, that reveals a special kind of bond between the two and can be a lot of fun to write.

6 **Super or Magical Powers:** Sometimes characters can have special powers, like Sabrina on *Sabrina the Teenage Witch* or Samantha in *Bewitched*. It is important to list the character's powers and the rules surrounding such powers so you will know how to use them consistently in the plot.

Now, let's look at the next important tool for developing characters:

Character Compass Traits

You must be able to see a character's world through his/her eyes because each character will have his/her own limited POV (point of view). Examine a character's personality to know how he/she will react in any given predicament. His/her traits serve as compass points and direct a character's choices and reactions throughout the journey. Ask yourself: what are the character's strengths and weaknesses? What motivates this particular character (power, love, fun, peace)? While sitcom characters often appear one or two-dimensional, truly great sitcom characters are just as layered as dramatic characters.

Let's examine the compass traits of the characters from *Everybody Loves Raymond:*

Ray (Father Doesn't Know Best)	Debra (Sensible Mom)	Robert (Lovable Loser)	Marie (Bossy)	Frank (Sarcastic-One-Liner)
Immature	Romantic	Insecure	Judgemental	No-Nonsense
Show-Off	Responsible	Loyal	Opinionated	Wise Cracker
Whiney	Nurturing	Loner	Protective	Loud
Lazy	Sympathetic	Courageous	Smug	Couch Potato
Cowardly	Smart	Fun-Loving	Nurturing	Sarcastic
Good Provider	Good Listener	Jealous	Manipulative	Crude
Insensitive	Bossy	Idealistic	Meddling	Old School
Easy-Going	Critical	Honorable	Great Cook	Always Hungry
Clueless	Frustrated	Low Self-Esteem	Smothering	Cranky
Irresponsible	Short-Tempered		Passive-Agressive	Cheap

These are just some of the traits these characters reveal and exude in the course of the series. Next time you view a program, start scrutinizing the characters. Get to know them as you would your own friends; that way, you'll be able to write them believably.

The Character Trinity

The most important factors to know about your character in regards to plot, whether the A-story or subplots, are:

1 His/Her Goal

2 His/Her Need

3 His/Her Fear

Think of these elements as the character trinity. You must create your driver (the A-story character) with a very blatant goal and need, then put him/her on a one way street to achieve it. Your driver's goal fuels the A-story while your character's need fuels the emotion. The character's goal and need are two distinct elements. This goal and need most often conflicts with the character's fear and/or is motivated by it. In addition, the character trinity will be interlinked with the story's springboard.

Let's take a look at our examples:

In *Everybody Loves Raymond,* "The Canister," Debra's goal is to sneak the canister back into Marie's house. Debra's need is to keep Marie from discovering she was right, because Marie finally apologized and treated Debra respectfully. Debra's fear is that Marie will find out the truth, and then she'll never have Marie's full respect again. Notice how the character trinity interweaves to build the story.

In *Friends,* "The One Where Joey Loses His Insurance," Joey's goal is to get an acting job while his need is to have insurance. His fear is that he will get hurt before his insurance is active again. The character trinity develops the episode's plot.

In *Fawlty Towers,* "Basil the Rat," Manuel's goal is to keep his pet "hamster" while his need is the companionship his pet brings him. His fear is that he will lose his pet. Fawlty's goal is in direct conflict: to get the hotel up to code before the health inspector comes. His need is to keep the hotel running. His fear is that the health inspector will close *Fawlty Towers,* especially if the inspector finds a rat on the premises.

The Character Arc

What a character learns in the course of the episode, story arc, and/or the series is called the character's arc. As I said before, while a sitcom character may learn something in the course of the episode, he/she will be back to his/her same old self next week.

In "The Checkbook," *Everybody Loves Raymond,* Ray learns that keeping up with the family's finances and balancing the checkbook is no easy task. He, however, does not suddenly become mature and responsible from that episode on. If he did, we'd lose much of the humor on the show.

Character Tics

It's always fun to create a character tic for one on your characters. A character tic is a trait or quirk unique to that particular character, like Sherlock Holmes's famous hat and pipe. Often tics are exhibited in voice distinctions. A character tic readily identifies a character to the audience. Always let a character's tic play into the plot whenever possible.

In *Just Shoot Me*, Dennis often sees and hears (as does the viewer) a little devil on his shoulder debating with a little angel on Dennis's other shoulder.

In *Newhart,* Daryl and other brother Daryl never speak, only their brother Larry does.

In *Will & Grace,* Jack often uses TV pop references as exclamations:

```
          JACK
You are so Markie Post in every single
Lifetime movie.


          JACK
Holy Anne Heche Laffon, he's straight!


          JACK
Jennifer Jason Leigh, these people are freaks.
```

In *Fawlty Towers,* Manuel the busboy speaks Spanish, and very little English which provides for a lot of great gags and jokes.

One popular character tic is to create a character that the audience never sees, but that the other characters know and talk about, like Nile's wife (now ex-wife) Maris on *Frasier* or Stanley on *Will & Grace*. The writers of *Home Improvement* used this tic in a unique way; neighbor, Wilson, was shown and heard, but with one exception, the viewer never fully saw his face. Be imaginative, and have fun with this device when developing one of your characters. Just remember, if you give them a tic, it's stuck with them for the course of the series.

Character Tags

Once you begin writing the actual script, there is a technical format to follow in regard to characters. When a new character steps onto the page for the first time, introduce his/her name in CAPS and sum him/her up in a one or two sentence character tag (description) which sticks in the reader's mind. You want a reader to immediately grasp who this character is. When you write for an existing series, you'll only write a character tag if you introduce a new character. If you are creating your own characters for an original series, you will have to use a character tag for every character you introduce in your pilot script. For example, possible character tags for these characters could be:

MARIE BARONE: 60's, yes, she's the mother-in-law from hell, but with good intentions—who just happens to live next door to her grown son and his wife. Pushy, always right, there's nothing she won't do for her two sons and daughter-in-law, most especially interfering with their lives on a daily basis. Of course, her overwhelming nurturing and smothering usually comes with a side order of spaghetti and meatballs, so life's not all bad in the Ray Barone household. *(Everybody Loves Raymond)*

JOEY TRIBIANNI: a struggling actor nearly thirty (that's 103 in actor years). Definitely not the brightest bulb in the chandelier, but his adorable smile, boyish charm, and cluelessness are a definite babe magnet for this New York Italian. *(Friends)*

SABRINA SPELLMAN: "As if she doesn't have enough to worry about, new-kid-in-town, Sabrina, finds out on her 16th birthday she's a witch. But eyes of newt and bubbling cauldrons can't always get her what she wants, a cool boyfriend and the respect of her high-school peers." While every teenager thinks that they're different and a freak, Sabrina, really is!" *(Sabrina the Teenage Witch)* *paraphrased from TV Guide; Fall Preview Issue, 1999.

Make each character sound original and distinctive in the tag. You'll use these tags later in your script, so do the work here. You don't want to slow your momentum during your first draft when you're focusing on plot.

Recap

1 Know each character's type, dipstick, and major compass traits. These will keep you writing the character consistently and aid you in knowing how the driver will react in each scene and/or situation. The characters must drive the plot on their own, not be bused by you, the writer.

2 Make sure each character you create is unique and fun. In addition, have him/her complement and contrast other characters in the script.

3 Make your characters relatable, not perfect. They must have flaws as well as enviable traits, especially in sitcoms.

4 Make your character tics unique and fun if you choose to create them.

5 Make your character tags memorable; sum up the essence of your character in the most fascinating and succinct way possible.

For ideas on developing intriguing characters, examine those characters from the classic sitcoms. These characters have endured the test of time and have been successful for a reason. They can give you a great sense of how to create unforgettable characters.

NOTE: In the exercises below, for those writing for an existing series, answer the character questions based on your observation of the series' characters for which you are writing. These exercises will help you learn more about the characters and help you get to know them better so that you can write them consistently and convincingly. For those writing an original pilot, do these exercises to create characters for your own series. These exercises demand a lot of your time and thought: do not do them all in one session! Work at your own pace. Whenever you feel tempted to rush, that's the time to stop and return to the exercise another day.

Exercise 9: Create a character dipstick for each main character (those existing or those you are creating) in the opening credits. Include the dipstick measuring marks 1–6, especially noting relationships and back story between the main characters.

Exercise 10: Now make a character compass for each of these characters. If creating your own original series, remember sitcom characters are flawed, that's where you'll derive much of the series humor. What is the character's popular sitcom type?

Exercise 11: Look for traits in the supporting cast which clash with the driver's traits to help develop humor and/or conflict in your story.

Exercise 12: From the six or twelve episodes you watched, write what the A-story character's goal, need, and fear is in each episode.

Exercise 13: For the episode you are writing, list your own driver's goal, need, and fear. Next, write what the character arc will be (if applicable). Include other goals by characters in the subplots, especially those in direct conflict with the A-story character's goal.

Exercise 14A: For those writing for an existing series, create a character tag for any new supporting characters you are introducing in your episode.

Exercise 14B: For those creating an original series, sum up your driver and any other supporting characters that you will use in your pilot script in a one to three sentence tag.

Chapter Seven
Sitcom Writing Fines

Sitcom fines are mistakes that leap off the page and shout, "amateur!" to the professional reader. When producers and/or executives read spec scripts, there are certain things they watch for. Make sure you follow the road rules below because you're beginning your sitcom career—you can't afford to be fined!

One of the most important factors producers watch for is to see if you truly know their show and their characters. In other words, they want to know if you've done your homework, so remember:

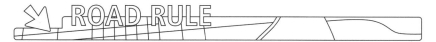

Road Rule #5: Don't break the rules of the series' sitcom world!

Whichever show you decide to write for, make sure you stick within the rules of its sitcom world; present yourself as a professional. You don't want to write an episode of *Everybody Loves Raymond* where Raymond cheats on his wife, because in this sitcom world, Raymond and Debra are happily married; regardless of their bickering, they truly love each other. Secondly, adultery isn't a laughing matter: this is a family tunnel, which means families watch the show. You want humor, not trauma. Likewise, if you're writing an episode for *Sabrina the Teenage Witch*, you'll have to stay in the rules of what's acceptable for her kind of powers and character. Sabrina will never intentionally harm someone with her magic, or use her powers for evil.

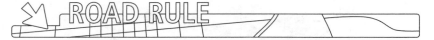

Road Rule #6: Limit crowd scenes.

Any script that presents difficulty or greater costs to producers will be "ticketed" for a huge fine. So forget selling your pilot script or getting a freelance assignment. As a television writer, you must think like a producer as well. Be aware of the financial ramifications of producing what you write, especially if you aren't writing for one of the Big Four (ABC, CBS, NBC, and FOX). Cable channels don't have tons of money to pour into original shows so don't knock yourself out of the market by writing an original series or sample script that demands hundreds of extras, or even fifty extras.

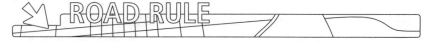

Road Rule #7: Don't add numerous new locations and/or new sets unless it is a rule of that particular sitcom world.

Sets for the TV series are established in the pilot episode and the episodes that follow. They are reused for time and cost efficiency. So use these sets and locations when you write your sample script. Adding new locations and new sets in a series is costly. So is writing a story in which a set is remodeled and/or destroyed. By using established sets and locations, your script already looks and reads professionally.

For example, if you're writing a *Frasier* sample episode, you'd use Frasier's kitchen, den, elevator/hallway, coffee café, and the radio station DJ set. This doesn't limit your creativity; you're just keeping your creativity within the boundaries of the sitcom. One new set is okay as long as it's not a lavish set. While you will occasionally watch episodes where Frasier stays in an exotic beach cabana or at wintery ski lodge cabin, these episodes are the exceptions and are written by established writers and producers. Remember, producers don't want to know if you can write an atypical episode, they want to know if you can give them a dynamite story that takes place in Frasier's den, radio room, or café set because that's the arena of their sitcom world.

Additionally, if you want to write an *Everybody Loves Raymond* episode, you'd keep most of your scenes in Ray and Debra's kitchen, den, or bedroom. You might also use Marie's kitchen and the Italian restaurant set. You can add another set or two, just be aware of the costs you're adding to the episode's production.

Study the sitcom for which you want to write your sample script. Know the series' sets and locations so you can develop a story that incorporates as many of these as possible so you can prove to producers that you know the series and respect its financial limitations. Don't create an episode which requires a dozen new locations and sets.

For those creating an original series, don't develop one which requires a cast of twenty characters traveling to exotic locales every week. You don't want to break any of these Road Rules for your sitcom pilot and suffer these fines either. Keep your sitcom as appealing as possible to network or studio executives. This means keeping costs low while coming up with a saleable series.

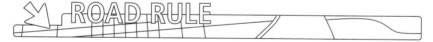

Road Rule #8: Don't kill off a series regular in your story!

While you may see an episode in which the characters experience death and/or attend a funeral, the sitcom isn't going to kill off someone the viewer is attached to. More likely, it's someone the audience has never met. This life event catalyst is always a great place to milk humor. In fact, one of the most famous episodes ever written, and touted as perhaps the most funny episodes of all, is the classic, "Chuckles Bites the Dust" episode from *The Mary Tyler Moore Show*. Viewers didn't know Chuckles the Clown, but when he's trampled by a rogue elephant who tried to shell Chuckles in his peanut uniform, it is one great joke after another. It also revealed how each of the characters dealt with death in a way true to their characters.

I know, some of you are saying, but what about "Abyssinia, Henry?" from *M*A*S*H*. In this famous farewell episode, Colonel Henry Blake was going home when his plane crashed and there were no survivors. This was a special circumstance: McClean Stevenson was leaving the show, the series producers wrote the episode, and *M*A*S*H* dealt with more serious issues due to its arena.

Thus, regardless of whether writing an original pilot and/or a sample script for an existing series, you don't want to be "ticketed." Have your scripts appear as professional as possible. Down the road, you will have greater flexibility once you have a track record with producers. For now, conform as much as possible in your own unique way.

Exercise 15A: If applicable, from the twelve episodes you recorded, write down all the rules in each of the two series that the characters follow in their sitcom world. List as many as you can observe.

Exercise 15B: If applicable, list all the rules you observe in the six episodes of the series you recorded. Next, if applicable list any special rules for the sitcom you are creating.

Exercise 16: In each episode you recorded, go back through the episode, and see how many sitcom fines, if any, occurred. If they did break several rules, check out the writing credit. Odds are the writer was the executive producer who can afford such fines.

Exercise 17: Next, create a log of locations and sets used in the episodes you recorded. In addition, for those, creating their own series, list the obvious sets and locales your series will use.

Chapter Eight
Graphing

The best way to learn the structure of a sitcom is by graphing numerous episodes. Writing down the structure of an episode, scene by scene, including the location of the scene, the time of day it occurs, who's in the scene, the dramatic beats of the scene, important information listed in the scene that's relevant to plots, and any line of dialogue that sums up the essence of the scene, is called graphing. It's best to record the episode you want to graph so that you can pause the recorded version while making notes. In addition, make a note of the real time the scene occurs in the episode just to get a sense of how many minutes (and pages) scenes average for that particular sitcom.

Below, I have included the graphs of two sitcom episodes which have aired on television. These are the graphs we'll discuss in subsequent chapters. I chose these particular episodes for several reasons:

1 They are accessible for study

2 They represent various TV tunnels

3 They follow the Writer's TV Road Map Structure

4 They are from a successful sitcom series

5 They were produced by different networks

NOTE: If you get a chance to record these graphed episodes when they rerun, do so. You can also probably find a fan of the series on the Internet who probably has every episode of a particular series taped. If so, ask the fan to dub you a copy for the price of the video tape and shipping. But don't worry—it isn't necessary to have seen these episodes to follow the examples.

Graph of *Everybody Loves Raymond*

"The Canister"

Central A-story Question: "Will Marie find out she was right about Debra still having the canister?"

Central B-story: "Will Debra and Ray be able to successfully sneak the canister back into Marie's house?"

TEASER: Ray's Kitchen: Allie and Ray color Easter eggs, Ray's competing with her. Marie drops in, asks Debra for the canister she loaned her. Debra says she returned it. (2 minutes)

MAIN CREDITS

ACT ONE

(1) Kitchen/Living Room: Robert joins them, warns mom that his dad has got into the ham. Marie persists about the canister, and Debra explodes, is Marie calling her a liar and a thief? She returned it and is hurt that Marie doesn't listen to her. Marie apologizes—a first! Then she leaves to check on the ham.

(2) Allie returns to the room with the canister; her mom gave it to her to keep her crayons in. Debra, Raymond, and Robert freak out! Raymond locks the door and closes the blinds.

(3) Ray says she has to return it, but Debra doesn't want to. For once, Marie finally apologized and validated Debra's feelings, the whole "balance of power shifted" and she doesn't want to give it back. If she goes down, they all will because from then on Marie will always be right about everything, using the canister incident to prove her point. They have to get rid of the canister!

(4) Robert and Ray don't want to because it was their Grammy's, but realize Debra's right about Marie lording it over them, and so agree.

(5-9) –writer did not use–

(10) GREEN LIGHT: Robert and Ray turn their backs as Debra tries to throw it away; it's as if she's burying a dead body. Debra looks at them—they're all in this lie together now. (12 minutes into episode)

Commercial Break

ACT TWO

(11) MIDPOINT/U-TURN: Living Room: Ray and Allie play video games on TV; Debra holds a pot of mashed potatoes ready to go to

Marie and Frank's. Suddenly, the canister rolls down the stairs, like a ghost toying with them. Ray gasps.

(12) Reveal Michael and Jeffrey run down the stairs to kick the canister again. Tell Debra they got it out of the trash when they were looking for Easter eggs. Ray says they must confess, Debra says, they will sneak it back in. Ray not enthusiastic about the idea, fearing they'll get caught.

(13) Marie & Frank's Living Room: Ray wears a parka, concealing the canister. Marie happy to see them, but worried because Ray's wearing a coat and it's hot. She thinks he's coming down with a cold. Debra attempts to get Marie out of the room so Ray can hide the canister, finally she succeeds.

(14) Ray looks for a place to put it and is caught by Robert who enters. He gasps, verbally jabs at Ray.

(15) Marie joins them and Robert rushes to hug Ray as Marie joins them. They hug, hiding the canister between them. She returns to the kitchen.

(16) Debra comes back out, yelling at them. She'll hide it; they need to go in the kitchen and keep Marie there. They exit.

(17) Debra tries to find a place for the canister when Frank enters and catches her. He laughs, she's doomed. Debra gives it to him and begs him not to tell Marie.

(18-19) -writer did not use-

(20) Suddenly, Marie enters and gasps. Frank says he had it—was keeping some nuts and bolts in it. Then when she made such a fuss about it missing, he decided to keep quiet as a joke. Marie's furious and he's in the doghouse now. Debra's touched because Frank took the heat for her.

(10½ minutes) Commercial Break

END TAG: Ray's Living Room—Marie brings them the canister, it holds bad memories now, wants to pass it on to Debra. Marie leaves, Debra can't accept it, what now—it's like guilt in a can. (1½ minutes)—End Credits

Graph of *Friends*

"The One Were Joey Loses His Insurance"

Friends

Central A-Story Question: "Will Joey get an acting job so his insurance will be reinstated?"

Central B-Story Question: "Will Ross succeed as a lecturer and get the professor appointment at NYU?"

Central C-Story Question: "Will Phoebe die at the end of the episode as the psychic predicted?"

Central D-Story Question: "Will Rachel find out she's still married to Ross?"

TEASER: Monica's Apt.: Rachel packs, Phoebe and Monica try to get Ross to tell Rachel that he still hasn't officially divorced her. Ross has interview for a job as a professor at NYU in the paleontology department. (2 minutes)

MAIN CREDITS

ACT ONE

(1) Central Perk: Phoebe informs the gang that a psychic told her that Phoebe had only a week to live. Ross practices his lecture on the group, it's awful. Chandler suggests that Ross open with a joke, or get some visual aids.

(2) Joey's Apt.: Chandler brings Joey a letter from SAG which tells Joey that his insurance has lapsed. Joey panics, now he has to be careful because he can't afford to get hurt. He has to get a job immediately! As he rushes out of the apartment, he runs into the door.

(3) Monica's Apt.: Rachel taking back candlesticks, Phoebe enters, complaining it's so exhausting waiting to die. Ross enters, his lecture went great, he brags.

(4) Talent Agency: Joey's agent, Estelle, yells at him for dropping her after she got him work; he says he never left her. She agrees to help

him find a job, but first must repair his reputation because "someone" has been bad mouthing him.

(5–8)—writer didn't use

(9) Joey's Apt.: Joey on floor in major pain as Chandler enters; Joey has hurt himself trying to get in shape for auditions, now he has this major bump coming out of his side.

(10) NYU lecture room: Ross lectures at NYU as Monica and Rachel drop by to surprise him. They stare at him in surprise as he gives his lecture using an English accent. Ross catches sight of them, and mutters, "Bloody hell." (12 minutes into episode)

Commercial Break

ACT TWO

(11) NYU lecture room: As class leaves, Ross explains quietly to Rachel and Monica that he was nervous about his speech, and somehow when he started talking, it was with a British accent—now he's stuck with it. Monica starts speaking with an Irish accent and Rachel with an Indian accent when Ross introduces them to another professor.

(12) Central Perk: Joey and Chandler, Joey in worse pain. He can't afford to go to the doctor, but Chandler says he'll loan him the money, just go. Phoebe arrives and says she'll go with Joey to the doctor.

(13) Ross upset, because he doesn't know what to do about the accent. Monica and Rachel suggest he just start phasing it out.

(14) Joey on audition: Joey in pain so he puts his hand in his pocket, but it looks like he's a pervert.

(15) Joey on another audition, this time for a dog commercial. They want him to pick up the heavy bag of dog food, he avoids it. They think he's being difficult and he doesn't get that job either.

(16) Joey on third audition: Need him to play a dying man in pain— he nails the job! (6 minutes)

Commercial Break

RESUME ACT TWO:

(17) Monica's Apt.: Rachel and Monica prank call Ross about the accent. Phoebe enters happily—her psychic reading was wrong, she isn't going to die—her psychic was the one who died.

(18) Studio: Chandler with Joey, Chandler had to help him get there he is in so much pain due to the hernia. It's the death scene in the hospital and Joey's character says goodbye to his son. The kid actor must cry on cue, but can't seem to find the tears. Joey's almost literally dying in pain—he just wants to do the scene and rush straight to the emergency room, but the kid keeps messing up.

(18A) Thirty-six takes later, Joey screams in pain, Chandler shows the kid Joey's hernia. The child actor starts crying and they get the scene.

(19) Rachel answers the phone and takes a message for Ross. It's the lawyer, she realizes she is still married to Ross and is furious.

(20) NYU lecture room: Ross tries to phase out the accent, but students wonder what's up. He admits to them he was nervous, and used the accent, but please grade him kindly when they fill out the evaluation card for him because he really wants to teach at NYU. He goes back to the lecture, but all his students want to do now is ask about the phony accent. Rachel storms into the room, upset, "What are you crazy?! I'm still your wife?!" Ross returns to his accent, "Allo, Rachel." (5½ minutes)

END TAG: Joey's Apt.: Phoebe and Joey, Phoebe is hitting him on the head as Chandler enters. He's all happy because he's got his insurance so he can get hurt now, and it's no problem. (½ minute)

In the graphs above, you'll notice that the writers didn't necessarily use all the streets available for their episode's story. That's because their story didn't warrant them. As you can see, fewer scenes were used in *Everybody Loves Raymond* than in *Friends*. Why? Because the *Everybody Loves Raymond* episode used only one subplot with its A-story while *Friends* dealt with three other subplots with its A-Story (due to the more ensemble storytelling).

When graphing, just mark the essence of the scene. If the scene intercuts (going back and forth) between two characters who are speaking on the phone, don't list each scene cut in your outline/ graph. Just list who's speaking and the point of the conversation. For example, in "Turkey Bowl" (*According To Jim*) all you'd write for one of the scenes is, "Jim and Cheryl on phone—when is he leaving the bowling alley and getting home to have Thanksgiving Dinner?!"

Okay, now it's time to practice some graphing on your own:

Exercise 18A: From the two series you previously viewed and recorded, graph the twelve episodes thoroughly; really familiarize you with each of sitcoms. List the A-story (the plot that dominates) and the subplot(s) within each episode. Be sure you have a central question listed for each of the plots in each episode.

Exercise 18B: For those writing an original pilot, graph the six episodes you recorded to familiarize yourself with the series for which you will write your second script. List the main plot (the story that dominates) and their subplot(s). Be sure you have a central question listed for each of the plots in each episode.

Chapter Nine
Introduction to Plot

Time to zoom into the fun and exciting world of plotting a sitcom story, starting with the basics:

Road Rule #9: Two script pages equal on average one TV screen minute if using video or four-camera film format. One script page equals on average one TV screen minute if using film format.

Thus, while you have 22 minutes to tell your half-hour story (plus 8 minutes of commercials) your sitcom script will range somewhere between 25–44 pages depending on whether it's tape or film format. Simply put, film format means the script is formatted like a typical screenplay: single spacing. Thus, your script will average one minute per page and be about 24 pages. Video tape format or four-camera film format (which means it's shot before a live audience) means that you will double-space your dialogue and all stage directions (for example: "STUNNED, ROBERT TURNS AROUND…") will be written in caps. In video tape format, an additional distinction is made: the stage directions will also be double spaced. This makes the read through and staging easier for actors when they first run through the script on the set.

To know which type of format a particular sitcom uses, you'll need to acquire a copy of one of the scripts. To better understand the four-camera film format which is generally used now, examine the script example in the appendix. You want your scripts to look professional, so:

Road Rule #10: Follow the standard industry script format!

This means, use a format of 52 lines per page with the 52 lines appearing between the top and bottom holes of your three-hole punched paper (brads in top and bottom holes only). That falls in the range of a .170-.172" in line height using the industry's standard font "Courier New." Don't try to jazz up your teleplay by using some funky font. You'll only look like an amateur who's trying to pull attention away from his story.

So do you fill all those blank pages? You begin with:

The TV Sitcom Writer's Road Map

Remember those numbers represent on the graphs you made? Your plots are a series of streets which merge into their respective Central (?) Avenues. Each street on the Road Map equals one scene or a sequence of dramatic beats (obstacles and/or dilemmas). You create a new scene each time you switch time (for example: going from afternoon to evening) or location (going from inside the lunchroom to outside the school). You create a new beat with a character moment, a character discovery, or an incident in the plot which shifts the lead character's goals and/or escalates the story's conflict.

Each set of ten streets or scenes/beats forms one city block of the episode. It takes two city blocks to construct your half-hour script. Thus:

Act One = 1 city block (introduces the A-story, any subplot(s) and any new characters; sets up who the plot(s) is/are about if the sitcom has more than one lead character, and builds conflict, ends with escalation or twist in the plot).

Act Two = 1 city block (continues with complications, character(s) struggles to solve the problem, and wraps up plot(s) in the climax and/or resolution. It can also set up a continuing thread or runner, generally ending in a cliffhanger.

In your construction, integrate the plots and the characters so that each is dependent on the other. The plot is your system of roadways and the character is the driver zooming down your story's streets. Within the first few streets, compel the audience to care about your driver's problem in the episode; then tow him/her into opposition.

Falling Rocks

You must include falling rocks (obstacles). These serve as the dramatic beats in the scene which heighten the tension in the plot. Each falling rock along the journey must cause your driver to react and keep him/her zooming forward in the story. To construct problems for your characters, you need to decide who or what is pushing those falling rocks off the cliff in front of them. Is it the situation, another character, or the driver him/herself that is causing the obstacles? With each new plot point or beat, your character must become more desperate to achieve his/her goal. In sitcoms, a character's goal may change, adjusting as he/she is hit by a falling rock. For example, in *Everybody Loves Raymond*, "The Canister," Debra's goal is to keep Marie from discovering Debra does have the canister. Midway through her goal shifts to sneaking the canister back into Marie's house (in order to keep her original goal).

Parallel Streets

They are your subplots which reflect and/or enhance the A-story plot. You have to weave these streets throughout your script, incorporating plot(s) for the supporting cast. Depending on your sitcom cast, you will have about 1–3 subplots to juggle with your main or A-story plot, with each subplot having about 2–5 plot beats. The subplots demand less screen time. For sitcoms such as *Friends* and *Seinfeld* where the subplots feature four or more of the lead characters, these plots are called thread plots, and the plots are more equally divided with the main plot. These subplots must merge with your A-story or with each other during the course of the episode.

In *Everybody Loves Raymond*, "The Canister," the subplot of Debra and Raymond trying to sneak the canister back into Marie's supports the main plot: Will Marie discover Debra still has the canister?

In *Friends*, "The One Where Joey Loses His Insurance," the subplot of Rachel discovering she's still married to Ross merges with the Ross professor plot in the climax of the B-story.

Your subplot(s) and your main plot in each city block must keep progressing the story as your characters drive toward the episode's climax. Your story's speed limit (tension) increases, compressing time shorter and shorter until real time for your characters often becomes reel time. This brings us to the need of the "ticking clock."

Ticking Clocks

A ticking clock is a story device which sets up tension and demands immediate action by the character(s). It dictates that a character(s) perform a certain action by a specific time or a grave consequence will occur. It is a major obstacle with a time limit attached. Often this device is set into motion by the story's antagonist (character in opposition with the lead character). A ticking clock(s) can help you plot your story. Where you set it in motion depends on your story's individual needs, but in sitcoms, it's usually found in the first few beats of Act One.

From "In Basil the Rat," *Fawlty Towers,* the health inspector sets off the ticking clock on the very first street: Basil has 24- hours to take care of the dozens of health code violations in his kitchen or the hotel will be shut down.

Rest Areas

This is a breathing space for your characters and for the viewer. These moments allow the characters to refuel before facing more falling rocks and dangerous curves, and also give the viewer a chance to relate more strongly with the character. The rest area is often a reflective moment for a character or can also be a comic relief scene. It is a beat in which there is no (or very little) plot advancement. In this beat, a character reveals more about him/herself.

In *Friends,* "The One Where Joey Loses His Insurance," Rachel and Monica prank call Ross about his fake accent.

In *Everybody Loves Raymond,* "The Canister," the rest area falls where Robert talks about the Marie Barone apology, and Debra expresses she's touched by Marie's acknowledgment of Debra's feelings.

In *Will & Grace,* "Leo Unwrapped," Jack dances gaily as he plays a video disco game while Grace rushes around the arcade looking for a bathroom.

In addition to all of the above, there are a couple of other factors to consider before you start plotting:

Elements Which Affect Plot

Certain factors within a sitcom series will affect how you plot your story:

- Breaking the 4th Wall
- Character Daydreams, Dreams, or Fantasizes
- Comedy
- Flashbacks or Flashforwards
- Music Montage
- Runners

1 Breaking the 4th Wall

This means the character(s) actually looks into the camera and speaks directly to the audience, and thus are breaking that fourth, unseen wall between the viewer and the character. This is a quick way to expose the true feelings of a character and reveal more about what is going on in his/her thoughts. In sitcoms, it's used to also add humor to the story.

Bernie Mac uses this plot gimmick as one of the rules within its TV world. If you write a sample spec for this series, you would have to incorporate this plot gimmick in your own story so you aren't breaking the rules of its sitcom world.

2 Character Daydreams, Dreams, or Fantasizes

Here, the audience is taken into the daydream, sleeping dream, or fantasy of a character. This generally allows the writer a good way to escape the rules of the TV world for that episode because in a dream or fantasy, you can go as wild and crazy as you want. These gimmicks are used for humor or to show profound insight about a character.

In "If Boys Were Girls," *Malcolm in the Middle*, a very pregnant Lois imagines what her and her husband's lives would have been like if they'd had four girls instead of four boys as they ponder on the gender of their next child.

3 Comedy

To quote a Hollywoodism: "While films are larger than life, sitcoms are smaller than life." Sitcoms tell stories of exasperated characters experiencing exaggerated events where the goals at stake are not life or death. They may feel like a life or death situation to a character, but they are just tiny moments in the character's life blown way out of proportion by comedy. Sitcoms don't deal with sobering issues, their stories are about everyday events and life moments which are exaggerated to the "-nth" degree. Generally, the character's goals are ridiculous and his/her schemes to achieve the goal are even more outrageous. This is what creates the humor in the episode.

4 Flashbacks or Flashforwards

This is when a character remembers something from his past, and "flashes" back. That is, the audience sees the character in the moment he is remembering. In this way, the audience gets to feel and experience the scene just as the character did. This can be funnier than just having a character tell about a past memory.

You can also flashforward in storytelling. This is when we see a character projected into his future. Often, this gimmick combines with daydream or fantasy as a character thinks about what will happen if s/he makes a certain choice, then the story flashforwards to show what the character believes will happen. This is a great way to develop visual humor.

Scrubs uses this gimmick as a rule of its sitcom world. The main character often flashes back or forward to mine humor as it depicts what Dorian is thinking and feeling.

For example, in the pilot episode of *Scrubs*, "My First Day," when the Chief of Staff asks Dorian a question on rounds, he flashes to the image of himself with antlers on his head in the dark of night as an eighteen wheeler comes barreling at him and he stands frozen in the headlight beams.

5 Music Montage

This is a series of shots and/or scenes shown as a song or music plays. Most often it is used to illustrate passage of time, but can also be used to help reveal a character. This gimmick evokes a mood and tone for the episode, and can really make a statement and hit an audience emotionally as well as add humor when used well.

Everybody Loves Raymond used this gimmick in "Italy" to reveal Raymond's reflection and change of mood as he stops pouting and starts to see the beauty of Italy.

6 Runners

Stories which aren't tied up within the episode, but are carried throughout the sitcom are called runners, continuing threads, or serialized stories. They may or may not be consecutively plotted. Most threads in a series are romance plots. For example, the storyline in *Frasier*: Will Daphne and Niles get together? Sam and Diane (*Cheers*) Ross and Rachel or Joey and Rachel (*Friends*) Winnie and Kevin (*Wonder Years*)… you get the idea.

Try these exercises.

Exercise 19: Go through your graphs and highlight all the falling rocks in each story, then list any ticking clock(s) in each (if applicable). Be sure it is a true ticking clock (a major obstacle with a time limit) and not just a falling rock (obstacle). Underline any rest areas depicted as well.

Exercise 20: Think about your own story and plots. Does the sitcom for which you are writing or creating use any of these five elements which affect plot? If every episode contains them, then you must use them, too. If the sitcom occasionally uses these elements, then you can too if you like.

Chapter Ten
The Teaser

Okay, time for the fun part: putting the characters into the plot. Most sitcoms start with a cold opening which "teases" the viewer into not switching the channel. This is known as the teaser. It can set up what the episode is about, reveal something more about a character, or just be played for the laugh.

Road Rule #11: Your first scene is crucial so think visually and humorously! Hook the viewer from the beginning frame and capture your first laughs here!

In your script, the Teaser will be your first 1–3 pages. Most often, the Teaser is followed by the sitcom's main credits and title logo, then the series breaks for a commercial. The Teaser exists to grab and hold the viewer's attention through the commercial break (and the reader's attention so that he'll keep turning those pages). For sitcoms, the Teaser must be funny and/or endearing.

Let's take a look at the Teasers from the graphed examples in this book:

In "The Canister," the story sets-up that it is Easter weekend. In Ray and Debra's kitchen, Marie drops over to ask Debra for the canister that she loaned her daughter-in-law. Debra vehemently insists she returned it as Raymond competes with his young daughter, coloring Easter eggs. *(Everybody Loves Raymond)*

This Teaser cues the viewer that the episode is going to be about the canister, provides humor from the character's personalities, and sets up the tension between Marie and Debra. It runs about two minutes. Main credits roll, then the story resumes after a commercial break.

In "The One Where Joey Loses His Insurance," the Teaser takes place in Monica's apartment. Rachel packs while Phoebe and Monica try to get Ross to confess to Rachel that he still hasn't officially divorced her. Ross promises to later, but informs them that he has an important interview for a job as a professor at NYU in the paleontology department. *(Friends)*

This Teaser reveals that Rachel is moving, sets up the B-story and the D-story. While it doesn't set-up the A-story (this is an ensemble cast, it doesn't have to) it does depict character relationships, and that a secret is waiting to explode in Ross's face (D-story). The Teaser raises the central questions: "Will Ross get the job? Will Rachel find out she's still married to Ross?" These questions invoke the viewer's attention and keep the viewer watching to see what will happen next. This Teaser runs about two minutes before the main credits roll, followed by a commercial break. Then, Act One continues.

If the sitcom for which you're writing doesn't begin with a Teaser, then you won't use one in your sample episode.

Try these exercises.

Exercise 21: Examine the six or twelve episodes you graphed earlier. List the beats of the Teaser: does the Teaser set up the main plot or any of the subplots?

Exercise 22: Fill in your springboard/premise and A-story central question on your Sitcom Road Map Form. Also copy the goal and need for the driver of your story onto the form. Next, list your Teaser.

Chapter Eleven
Act One

The first city block on your Sitcom Road Map forms Act One. This is where you introduce this week's set-up/predicament and who this particular episode will focus on if the sitcom is a duo lead, like in *Will & Grace,* or an ensemble like in *Friends.* Act One is also where you will introduce a new character if applicable, but most likely you'll just be continuing and/or expanding character relationships.

In Act One, you must establish the story in the most fascinating way possible without giving away your plot. What new problem or opportunity is the character going to face or pursue? What crazy efforts will the character undertake to solve the problem or take advantage of the opportunity at hand? His/her outrageous actions (which are generally inappropriate) are what will escalate the plot.

NOTE: For those creating an original pilot, this is where you will also establish the sitcom's arena (setting) and characters, expanding upon the locale(s) and characters you introduced in the Teaser.

In addition, setup any subplot(s) and hurl some falling rocks (obstacles) toward your main character. Remember, Act One can also be a great place to set up a ticking clock to drive the tension throughout the episode. Then, at the end of Act One, you'll create the dramatic beat that really escalates or twists your story's plot.

Thus, Act One will contain two important plot points: the Tow-Away Zone and the Green Light.

Tow-away Zone— The Catalyst

The first important plot point in Act One is the catalyst which should come somewhere between page one and five of your sitcom script. On your Road Map, it falls within the first few streets (1st—2nd Street). This street is where your driver is towed or pulled into the story. It's what spins each plot line and sets up each story's central question, the A-story, the B-story, the

C-story, etc… For the A-story, this scene is found in the Teaser or by the second beat on the Road Map. You have 22 minutes to tell the story, you can't waste time setting up the plot. A subplot or two may also be set-up, either in the Teaser or in the opening scenes of Act One.

In *Everybody Loves Raymond,* "The Canister," the Tow-Away Zone for the A-story is when Allie bounces into the living room with the canister—Debra gave it to her for a crayon box. Debra, Raymond, and Robert freak out! (2nd Street).

This dramatic beat in the opening scene of Act One spins the A-story's central question: "Will Marie find out she was right about Debra still having the canister?"

In *Friends,* "The One Where Joey Loses His Insurance," the catalyst for the A-Story is when Chandler brings Joey a letter from SAG which tells Joey that his health insurance has lapsed. Joey panics, now he has to be careful because he can't afford to get hurt. He has to get a job immediately! (2nd Street). This spins its central question: "Will Joey find an acting job so his insurance will be reinstated?"

If you have a subplot, you'll have a catalyst for it as well, although it may or may not be shown on screen. For example, the catalyst for the C-story in the episode above is when the psychic tells Phoebe that she will die within the week. This scene takes place off scene, but is related to the group by Phoebe which then spins the C-story central question: "Will Phoebe die at the end of the episode as the psychic predicted?" (Yeah, yeah, we know she won't, this subplot is strictly for humor.) This occurs on 1st Street of the Sitcom Road Map. Likewise, the catalyst that sets up the question: "Will Ross succeed as a lecturer and get the professorship at NYU?" occurs in the interview which is also played off screen.

The Green Light—Major Escalating Plot Beat

Here, your driver (lead character) zooms into the action. Maybe he/she doesn't want to drive into the action, but commits to the conflict nevertheless. On this street beat, one of your drivers is hurled a crisis and/or dilemma, and sometimes must make a choice in regards to the plot.

In addition, on 9th or 10th Street, there must be more at stake and/or more emotional impact than before for your driver. The Green Light beat marks the end of Act One and precedes the commercial break; thus, it must be compelling enough to keep viewers from changing the channel.

In *Everybody Loves Raymond,* "The Canister," the Green Light falls on 10th Street when Robert and Ray turn their backs as Debra tries to throw it away; it's as if she's burying a dead body. Debra looks at them—they're all in this lie together now. (12 minutes into episode)

In *Friends,* "The One Where Joey Loses His Insurance," the Green Light for the A-story appears on 9th Street: Joey's hurt himself trying to get in shape for auditions, and now he has this major bump coming out of his side—a hernia. (10 minutes into episode)

Story Signposts

To ensure that your 9th or 10th Street is strong enough to keep the viewer from switching channels during the commercials, follow the signposts below:

1	**GO**	Hurl a crisis, dilemma, and/or choice at the driver of the plot.
2		Keep viewers guessing about the outcome of the central question.
3	DETOUR	Shift the story down a new road.
4	DANGER AHEAD	Make the road (plot) more hazardous for the driver.
5	TUNNEL	Next Act This Exit: Speed the story into the next act.
6	STOP GO	End/begin the act out on a humorous note!

NOTE: Some of these signposts are derived and/or adapted from the turning point's functions Linda Seger lists in her book *Making A Good Script Great,* a marvelous book on screenwriting.

Let's review our sample episodes to see how the writers developed these signposts to create their respective Green Light Scenes:

In *Everybody Loves Raymond,* "The Canister" episode used nearly all of the signposts to make an effective act break:

(1) Debra has been hurled a crisis earlier in the scene, now she is hurled a dilemma: does she admit to Marie she was wrong and give back the canister, or throw it out and never tell Marie? Debra makes the choice to throw the canister away, never telling Marie. Ray and Robert relent and make the choice to go along with her, keeping her secret.

(2) It does keep the audience guessing—will Marie find out?

(3) It doesn't shift the story down a new road, the catalyst did that.

(4) It does, however, make the road more hazardous—there's a secret just waiting to be exposed.

(5) It definitely speeds us into the next act as the audience eagerly waits to see what will happen if Marie finds out.

(6) It leaves viewers laughing because the scene is written as if Debra's getting rid of a dead body instead of a canister.

In *Friends,* "The One Where Joey Loses His Insurance," the signposts are met in this manner:

(1) Joey's hurled a crisis: he's injured himself just when he needs to be in top shape for auditions. Joey makes the choice to audition anyway.

(2) The audience now wonders what will happen on the auditions, so it does keep viewers guessing.

(3) It shifts the story onto a new road, because now it looks like Joey will not be able to get an acting job.

(4) It makes the road more hazardous because it's going to be difficult for Joey to nail the audition when he's in so much pain.

(5) It speeds the audience into the next act as the viewer waits to see if Joey will succeed.

(6) It's a funny escalation of the A-story, especially as Chandler reacts to the large bulge growing out of Joey's abdomen.

The City Block of Act One

Look again at the graphs in this book and examine their first city blocks to see which plot lines were established, and how much story time each one dominates.

In *Everybody Loves Raymond,* "The Canister," sets up the A-plot:

Debra-canister plot = 1st-10th Streets (with beats 5–9 unused)

This city block establishes who the episode is going to focus on, Debra, and introduces that it's Easter weekend and they'll be having a family dinner for the holiday. This whole city block runs approximately 10 minutes.

In *Friends,* "The One Where Joey Loses His Insurance," sets up four plot lines:

Joey insurance plot (2nd, 4th, 9th Streets)

Ross professorship plot (Teaser, 1st, 3rd, 10th Streets)

Phoebe dying plot (1st, 3rd Streets)

Ross and Rachel still married plot (Teaser)

(5th—8th beats unused)

The first city block establishes the A–D storylines. As you can see the Joey insurance plot (A-Story) and the Ross professor subplot (B-story) take up most of the story while the Phoebe dying and Ross-Rachel marriage subplot form the smaller subplots, the latter carrying on the popular series runner: "Will Ross and Rachel finally get together?" This city block runs approximately 10 minutes.

As I mentioned at the beginning of this chapter, Act One will also include several falling rocks for your character(s) to build the plots. These obstacles may be set into motion by the driver, another character, and/or a antagonist.

Let's look at the falling rocks used in the Act Ones of our graphed examples:

In *Everybody Loves Raymond,* "The Canister":

First obstacle: Debra's pride keeps her from admitting her mistake and serves as an emotional obstacle as Debra wants to keep this "shift of power" on her side. (3rd Street)

Second obstacle: Ray and Robert don't want to get rid of the canister because it holds fond memories for them; she must convince them to lie to their mother. (4th Street)

Third obstacle: Debra gets rid of the canister—now a lie exists within the family just waiting to be discovered. (10th Street)

The last falling rock serves as an escalation in the plot as now a lie/secret exists which the three must keep.

In *Friends,* "The One Where Joey Loses His Insurance," obstacles for the A-story and B-story are:

First obstacle: Ross practices his lecture to the group—it sucks. He's sensitive about it. (1st Street)

Second obstacle: Joey's agent has badmouthed him because she thought he had dropped her, so she must do damage control to get him an audition. (4th Street)

Third obstacle: Joey injures himself while working out for his auditions. (9th Street)

Fourth obstacle: After bragging about how well his lectures are going and how he didn't use any gimmicks, Ross is caught using a phony British accent.

While the two episodes above did not use a ticking clock, if your plot needs one, set it up in Act One so it can help develop tension for your story.

The Recap

Act One contains the Tow-Away Zone and the Green Light. The main Tow-Away Zone is the catalyst which spins the A-story of the episode and its central question, occurring somewhere in the first few streets of Act One. Each subplot, however, will also have its own catalyst as well.

The next plot point, the Green Light, generally falls on the 10th Street On-Ramp, but possibly on 9th Street. It's the scene in which your driver must face a choice, crisis, and/or dilemma. It must incorporate most or all of the six story signposts in order to be effective enough to hold the viewer's attention through the commercial break.

Act One is the setup and beginning escalation of the episode's story using a few falling rocks and possibly a ticking clock. Altogether, Act One will run approximately 10–12 minutes, and usually comprises the first 19–22 pages of your script if using the four-camera film or video format.

Here are some exercises.

Exercise 23: Examine the six or twelve episodes you graphed earlier. List the A-Story's Tow-Away Zone. Did the main Tow-Away Zone fall within the Teaser? If not, on what street did it occur?

NOTE: Think about the A-story's central question. What is being answered in the climax of the episode? Only the scene that zooms your driver into that direction can qualify as the catalyst of the A-story.

Exercise 24: Next, list the Green Light beat of each episode. What time did they occur? Note how many of the signposts they each used on 9th or 10th Street. A strong act out will encompass 5–6 signposts. How long was each episode's Act One?

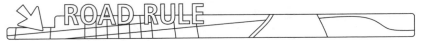

Exercise 25: From the six or twelve episodes you graphed, list each of their subplot(s) if applicable, in their respective Act Ones. How many plots did each episode set up? Which plot served as the A-story? Are any runners (continuing stories not wrapped up in the episode)?

Sitcom Road Map (see inlay page 206)

Remember, each street represents one scene or dramatic beat. Write a phrase or sentence per street to break down point of each scene or dramatic beat. As you construct your plot, keep in mind:

Road Rule #12: Your character must leave each scene needing more than when he/she entered it!

This is what assists you in developing tension within your plots so follow this Road Rule as you construct your story.

NOTE: As you block out Act One, you might not need to fill in every street on your Sitcom Road Map. That's okay. Sitcoms that are heavy on dialogue and have few scene changes like *Everybody Loves Raymond* will use less scenes/beats than those series heavy on plot gimmicks such as flashbacks or multiple sets like *Scrubs* or *Malcolm in the Middle*. Only use the streets (scenes/dramatic beats) your story requires, no more, no less.

Exercise 26: Next, create your A-Story Tow-Away Zone. Then, fill in your Green Light beat on 9th or 10th Street. Make sure your driver's goal is serviced by the two major plot points of Act One. Make sure your Green Light beat answers 5–6 story signposts for a strong act break.

As you juggle the main plot and its subplot(s) make sure each has a few falling rocks and/or a ticking clock to increase the tension. Keep raising the incline that your characters have to drive on.

Exercise 27: List any subplot(s) you want to construct. They will each have their own Tow-Away scene. With this in mind, it should be easy for you to fill in the rest of the streets for Act One on your Sitcom Road Map. Use the A-story central question to keep on track for your main plot.

Chapter Twelve
Act Two

Act Two consists of about 18–22 pages if writing for the four-camera film or tape format, averaging somewhere between 10–12 minutes of TV screen time and comprises 11th–20th Streets on your Sitcom Road Map. This act is about merging plots together in the climax and resolution of the episode. Thus, you'll continue to weave the A-story plot with the other plots, merging plot lines on 20th Street (if applicable). The writers of *Seinfeld* were masters at merging seemingly unrelated, insane, and inane plots into the climax. Some sitcoms, however, do not merge their plots. These sitcoms prefer to wrap each story up individually and are most often sitcoms that have ensemble leads, such as *Friends*. Follow whatever the sitcom normally does.

Each street in this block, just as in Act One, must lead into its respective Central (?) Avenue. As the characters travel these roads, they each must have enough "falling rocks" or obstacles to complicate Act Two. The story constantly rises up a steep incline by heightening the jeopardy and making the driver's road difficult to navigate. You must keep building upon the plots set up in Act One, escalating your story's tension into a hilarious and frenzied climax. This is how you keep these 18–22 pages interesting and humorous.

Act Two consists of three construction areas: the u-turn, the climax, and the resolution. If you have a runner as one of your subplots, then you might set-up some storylines for the next week in an optional cliffhanger. Nevertheless, you'll construct Act Two by opening with its first major plot point:

The U-Turn

The U-Turn appears on 11th Street and turns the story into an unexpected or opposite direction. It is the major plot point of Act Two, and the first scene after the commercial break of Act One. Sometimes, a discovery is made or a secret is revealed here. This midpoint occurs between pages 19–23 of your script. It must set up the action of Act Two and be funny enough to fuel the second half of the episode with humor. It does so by using the story signposts. For example:

In *Everybody Loves Raymond,* "The Canister," the U-Turn occurs as Debra and Ray start to go to his mother's house for Easter dinner. Suddenly, the canister stumbles down the stairs and Ray gasps.

It's a great U-Turn. Look at the story signposts it encompasses:

(1) It hurls a crisis, dilemma, and choice at the Debra and Ray. Now what? They decide to sneak it back into Marie's house without her knowing.

(2) Viewers are definitely guessing about the outcome.

(3) Shifts the story down a new road. Will they get caught sneaking it back, and be humiliated?

(4) Makes the road more dangerous because if they're caught, Marie will never let them forget it!

(5) Speeds the story, fueling Act Two with potential humor.

(6) It definitely opens the Act with humorous reactions from the characters as a discovery is made.

In *Friends,* "The One Where Joey Loses His Insurance," the U-Turn services the B-story; that's okay, as it is an ensemble series. Here,

Rachel and Monica surprise Ross at his lecture, only to end up surprised themselves—Ross is talking with a really bad British accent.

(1) It hurls a crisis and choice at Ross; he's surprised by Rachel and Monica, embarrassed to explain his phony accent. He doesn't know how to get rid of it without looking like an idiot, but he doesn't want to keep up the charade of being British.

(2) Viewers are definitely guessing about the outcome. How will Ross solve his problem?

(3) Shifts the story down a new road. It makes him face the problem, because now Rachel and Monica know his secret.

(4) Makes the road more dangerous because he doesn't want to admit he's a phony, he wants to get the professorship.

(5) Speeds the story, fueling Act Two with potential humor.

(6) It opens the Act on a humorous note as Ross's secret is revealed.

The U-Turn on 11th Street zooms the character into the motion of the episode, driving him/her toward the story's climax. The final crash (confrontation) at the end of Act Two is now inevitable. The question set up on the A-story, B-story, C-story... Central (?) Avenue will be answered soon as Act Two speeds towards its climax, hitting a few bumps along the way.

The City Block of Act Two

What obstacles occurred in our respective Act Twos?

Everybody Loves Raymond, "The Canister," presents four obstacles:

First Obstacle: Canister reappears. (11th Street)

Second Obstacle: Marie won't leave the living room so Ray can hide the canister; she's worried he has a cold since he's wearing a parka. (13th Street)

Third Obstacle: Robert enters and catches Ray with the canister. (14th Street)

Fourth Obstacle: Frank catches Debra trying to hide the canister. (17th Street)

Friends, "The One Where Joey Loses His Insurance," uses five obstacles to complicate the A-story and the B-story:

First Obstacle: Rachel and Monica find Ross using a phony British accent to deliver his lecture. (11th Street)

Second Obstacle: Joey's in so much pain, he doesn't know how he's going to audition. (12th Street)

Third Obstacle: Ross doesn't know how to lose the accent without jeopardizing his pride and his chance to get the professorship. (13th Street)

Fourth Obstacle: Joey's hernia makes him look like a pervert on the first audition and he can't lift the dog food on the second audition so he doesn't get the jobs. (14th & 15th Streets)

Fifth Obstacle: Child actor keeps blowing the scene because he can't cry. (18th & 19thA Streets)

Okay, now it's time for the story (or literary highway) to end.

The Climax

The climax is the scene viewers anticipate throughout the episode. It's the story arc. Most often the climax occurs on 20th Street, but it doesn't have to. Let your story and the graphs of the series for which you are writing guide you. Almost always a secret or discovery is revealed in the climax of sitcoms because obviously there is no going back: one can't un-reveal a secret and/or unlearn a discovery once it is known.

Let's look at the final crash or clash in these episodes:

In *Everybody Loves Raymond,* "The Canister," the U-Turn occurs as Frank is caught holding the canister and takes the blame for having it.

In *Friends,* "The One Where Joey Loses His Insurance," the climax is Ross confesses to the class he was nervous and the accent just fell off his tongue. He's not British, but he still hopes his students will evaluate him favorably because he really wants to teach at NYU and he's really a nice guy. Just then, Rachel storms in, screaming at Ross, "What are you crazy?! I'm still your wife?"

Notice above how the D-story merges with the B-story and sets up next week's episode with:

The Cliffhanger

The cliffhanger is an optional plot point found with the climax of the episode. Here, the character drives off the cliff and is left suspended in mid-air, so to speak, until the following week's episode. In other words, you hurl the driver into a mess of impending doom that won't be resolved until the opening of the next week's episode. The cliffhanger teases an audience into remembering to watch and tune into the sitcom the following week to see how the driver escapes the peril. Sometimes you'll need it, sometimes you won't. For example, in *Everybody Loves Raymond,* "The Canister," the writers didn't need or use a cliffhanger, but *Friends* did:

In "The One Where Joey Loses His Insurance," the cliffhanger is what will happen to Ross now that Rachel knows they're still married.

NOTE: Most often, a commercial will fall within Act Two, but you don't need to worry about this for now. If you have strong enough plot beats/obstacles in your Act Two, the producers can easily find the right place to take the commercial break.

Exercise 28: List the 11th Street U-Turn, for each of the six or twelve episodes you graphed. How did this scene turn the story in an unexpected direction?

Exercise 29: Next, list all subplots (if applicable). On which street in Act Two did they occur? Did each subplot add at least one obstacle to build its story?

Exercise 30: On the Sitcom Road Map, list your 11th Street U-Turn. Be sure it sends your character and story skidding into a new and/or unexpected direction. Use all the story signposts to be sure your U-Turn is funny enough to fuel the humor for Act Two.

Exercise 31: From the six or twelve episodes you graphed, list the climaxes of the various plots. Do these episodes use cliffhangers? If yes, what is it?

Exercise 32: Now go through your Sitcom Road Map, and fill in the rest of your Act Two, including the climax and/or cliffhanger, and merge the necessary plots. If you have subplots, remember, they will be more evenly distributed if you're writing for an ensemble lead sitcom. Make sure your story escalate by adding strong obstacles. Use a ticking clock if your story demands one.

NOTE: DO NOT skip these exercises. It's important to see how each episode escalates its plots before you map your own Act Two.

Chapter Thirteen
End Tag—The Resolution

The resolution simply completes the story and is used to getting the last laughs of the episode. It closes the plot(s) and allows the characters to absorb what has happened to them. The resolution generally falls in the end tag which is the scene after the last commercial break of the episode. If the sitcom's credits run on half a screen while the end tag of the episode is played on the other half of the screen, then you'll mainly stick with visual gags and not too much dialogue. The end tag occurs between pages 37–44 of your script and is your last scene.

In "The Canister" episode of *Everybody Loves Raymond,* the resolution is that Marie gives Debra the canister, and while she accepts it reluctantly, she confides in Raymond that she feels too guilty to enjoy it.

This scene lasts almost two minutes and the jokes are found strictly in the dialogue. It serves as a rest area as Debra and Ray reflect on the day.

In the *Friends* episode, "The One Where Joey Loses His Insurance," the resolution is Joey gets his insurance and now he can live life on the edge again.

This involves a visual gag as we see Phoebe hitting Joey in the head with a bat (he wears a helmet) on one half of the screen and end credits running on the other half.

A couple of exercises.

Exercise 33: From the six or twelve episodes you graphed, list the resolution presented in the end tag. Does the humor derive from mostly visual gags or dialogue jokes?

Exercise 34: Fill in your end tag resolution on your Sitcom Road Map. Be funny!

The Pit Stop Principle

Give yourself a round of applause! You just outlined your first sitcom! Now it's time for a Pit Stop.

Exercise 35: Don't touch your Sitcom Road Map. In fact, don't even think about your story for at least one week!

Yes, I know you're eager to start writing your episode and continue to the next chapter, but trust me, taking several days off from your story will save you tons of rewriting later. You've done an enormous amount of prep work, so take a bow. You've earned this writer's break.

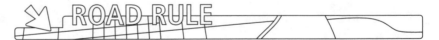

Road Rule #13: Never zoom past a Pit Stop. Pull over and refuel your creativity!

A Pit Stop allows everything you've read, written, and created in these past thirteen chapters to be absorbed into your thought processes. When you go through your first checklist in the next chapter, you want to do it with a fresh outlook and renewed energy. Not rushing at this point will save you a great amount of tuning-up (restructuring) later. So close the book, go have some fun, let the jokes marinate in your mind, and I'll see you in a week.

Chapter Fourteen
Checkpoint Charlie

Okay, you've taken a Pit Stop (No cheating! Only proceed if you have set your Sitcom Road Map aside for at least a week) and you're ready to go forward with a clear, refreshed, and objective mind. This beat outline is where you want to catch your structure mistakes, not in your half-hour script where you'll have 37–45 pages to muddle through. Therefore, take this chapter seriously and really examine your Sitcom Road Map for any flaws.

Start with this exercise.

Exercise 36: Using the criteria below, scrutinize your beat outline. Does your Sitcom Road Map pass every checkpoint listed? If you answer no to any question, then you've wandered off plot. Rework any beats or scenes necessary in your Sitcom Road Map.

1 Is your Teaser (opening) a grabber, hooking the viewer from the first scene and making them laugh?

2 Does your main Tow-Away (1st or 2nd Street) set up the A-story Central Question Avenue? Have you created Tow-Away Zones for each of your subplots?

3 Have you given your driver(s) a blatant goal and need in the episode? (Remember, the goal may change slightly as the character adjusts to the obstacles in the plot.)

4 Is your driver(s) actively driving along his/her plotted streets? He/she can't be a passenger in the story! And if you've created a guest starring character, make sure your lead character is still the lead!

5 Does your driver "hit the gas" and zoom into the plot at the Green Light (9th or 10th Street)? Is your driver hurled a crisis, dilemma, and/or choice?

6   Does your 9th or 10th Street incorporate 5–6 story signposts? Is it compelling enough to hold the viewer's attention throughout the commercial break?

7   Is the antagonist's goal and/or need in opposition with your driver's goal and need?

8   Do your subplots (if applicable) reveal the scope of the whole episode? Do they effectively set-up Act Two?

9   Does your 11th Street U-Turn (midpoint) speed the driver and/or story in an unexpected or opposite direction? Does your 11th Street incorporate 5–6 story signposts? Make sure it does so that it is strong enough to fuel the humor and action of the second half of the episode.

10 On 11th Street U-Turn, is there more at stake, more emotional impact for your driver than before?

11 On your 11th Street, is there no going back once the character commits to the plot? Does it set into motion the episode's climax?

12 Highlight the falling rocks you have created on your Sitcom Road Map. Do you have sufficient obstacles to sustain Act One and Act Two?

13 Is your story's incline (jeopardy) rising? Are each of your plots escalating effectively for your Act Two?

14 If you have a ticking clock, is it ticking?! Did you truly set it into motion?

15 Are your character(s) commitments rising as well?

16 Is the episode's climax bigger and funnier than the rest of the humor in your story? It must be!

17 Do you wrap up the A-story and any other plots necessary in the End Tag? Is your End Tag humorous leaving the audience chuckling?

18 If applicable, is your Cliffhanger strong enough to pull in the audience for the following week? Make sure it does.

19 Do these plots compel the audience to care about your characters and their predicaments?

20 Is any beat/scene on your outline just duplicating another beat/scene? If so, cut one of them. It's littering your literary highway.

If you answered yes to every question above, then you should be confident that each city block is building and leading into the story's climax. As long as your 10th and 11th Streets each accomplish 5–6 story signposts, speeding your plot(s) toward the answer to your Central (?) Avenue, then you are ready for the exercise below. Get ready to turn all that hard work into some creative fun.

Exercise 37: Write your Teaser, the opening of your episode. Remember, it must be funny! Setup any stories, here, if you want, or you can just play for character layering and laughs. Whichever, be sure you create an opening that compels the reader and viewer to stick with the character and his upcoming predicament.

NOTE: For those writing an original pilot, you will need to begin setting up your locale and your characters here. Be as succinct and humorous as possible.

Chapter Fifteen
Make 'em Laugh

The most important factor in sitcoms is, "make 'em laugh, make 'em laugh, make 'em laugh." As a sitcom writer, your job is to continuously fill the television screen with something comical and absurd. No matter what comedic style, the rule of thumb is:

Road Rule #14: Always yield to humor. If the joke is truly hysterical, then forget story logic and go for the laugh!

While your goal is always to write great visual and verbal gags, you want the humor to derive naturally from the plot and/or character.

Road Rule #15: The comedy must play to the scene! Use it when you can to move the story, but always play it to the scene.

Don't worry. Writing comedy is not so intimidating if you follow the comedy cones that follow.

Comedy Cones

Think of these as mechanisms of humor. Whereas traffic cones signal caution, comedy cones signal jokes and gags. Comedy cones can assist you in creating humor for your script. Drop them numerously along the streets of your sitcom.

- Blue Humor
- Characters In Drag
- Food Gags
- Hot Topics
- Musical Numbers
- One-Two-Payoff
- Parody
- Physical Gags and Pratfalls
- Play A Character Opposite of What's Expected
- Play A Visual Opposite of the Dialogue
- Potty Humor
- Props
- Rule of Three
- Running Gags
- Setup, Then Payoff
- Shock Value/Surprise
- Titles
- Try-Fails

1 Blue Humor

This is risqué humor, in other words, jokes about sex. This comedy cone is very popular on sitcoms because it's easy to go for the sex joke. Certain sitcoms will use this comedy cone more than others, especially those sitcoms that fall in the second hour of primetime.

A song plays as Jack and Karen have brunch:

> JACK
> Are you okay, Kar? You haven't touched your
> Jackaccino?
>
> KAREN
> Oh, it's just this song. Stan always put it
> on whenever we were making love. I call it
> his minute waltz.
> —*Will & Grace*

In "Traffic School," Robert wants to practice teaching his traffic
school class, but Frank and Ray rush to escape. Marie offers to make
Frank a cheese sandwich if he'll stay and listen to Robert. Reluctantly,
he gives in. Debra tries to coax Ray into staying:

> DEBRA
> I'll make you a grilled cheese sandwich. But
> it'll have to be with jelly because we're out
> of cheese.
>
> RAY
> Forget jelly, it'd have to be made out of…
> sex.
> —*Everybody Loves Raymond*

2 Characters In Drag

Sitcom characters that cross-dress are sure to get a laugh. There's just
something innately silly about men in dresses, and so much humor
to be extracted from such a character. It can be a running gag in the
episode or just a one time occurrence.

One of the classic drag characters from a sitcom is Corporal Klinger
from *M*A*S*H*, who continually wore women's clothes in hopes of
getting a Section 8, and thus discharged from the army.
—*M*A*S*H*

Likewise, on *The Drew Carey Show*, Drew's brother, Steve, is a cross-
dresser.

Bosom Buddies played half its series in drag as the two main
characters had to pose as women in order to afford the lower rent at
an all women's housing building.

In "Foreign Affairs," Suzanne makes Anthony dress up and pose as her maid, Consuela, in order to take the Naturalization exam and interview so Consuela can stay in the country.
—*Designing Women*

3 Food Gags

This type of gag is always popular, although more likely found in the animated sitcoms. This includes crazy food concoctions, food fights, or anything funny you can do with food.

Hal keeps fattening up Lois's supposedly low-calorie food by adding syrups, cream, and such. She becomes upset that she's gaining so much weight with her pregnancy.
—*Malcolm in the Middle*

One of the most classic food gags is when Joey puts his head up the uncooked Thanksgiving turkey and it gets stuck.
—*Friends*

Suzanne chats away, pouring milk into her coffee. She takes a sip as Charlene enters, looking for her "expressed" breast milk.
—*Designing Women*

4 Hot Topics

This comedy cone mocks hot topics or current events.

In "The Needle and the Omelette's Done," Will and Karen get Botox injections, using this popular trend of ridding wrinkles as a subplot and an arena from which to derive the jokes.
—*Will & Grace*

In "Big Haas and Little Falsie," Mary Jo ponders breast implants, a very current topic, then and now. It spun some fabulous humor.
—*Designing Women*

5 Musical Numbers

Having a character break into song and dance unexpectedly is a great comedy cone. Musical numbers or montages can also add humor as well as move the story along in a fun way.

In *Will & Grace,* Jack often breaks into song and dance; the sitcom also uses musical montages often.

In "Dancing With Debra," Ray reluctantly swing dances to avoid the wrath of Robert and Debra.
—*Everybody Loves Raymond*

In "The Nanny," the nanny randomly breaks out into the Warner Bros. tune, having previously worked for years at the studio.
—*Curb Your Enthusiasm*

6 One-Two-Payoff

This gag incorporates an action-reaction, and then an unexpected action. This technique builds tension because it creates a subconscious suspicion with the audience which the sitcom writer plays for humor. The setup is the one-two which can be played out as many rounds as you have time for, then the payoff comes. For example:

In the "Pilot" of *Malcolm in the Middle*:

(1) Malcolm's hit in the head with a milk cartoon. He yells at Spath, calling him an asshole. (action - reaction)

(2) Spath brings up his fists, desperate to delay the inevitable, and Malcolm hurls pudding in Spath's face. (action - reaction)

(3) Spath swings wildly at Malcolm who ducks the blow. (action - reaction)

(4) Spath stumbles and barely taps Stevie who turns his wheelchair over to make it look like Spath hit him. (payoff - unexpected action)

This turns all the kids against Spath because they think he punched a crippled kid.

7 Parody

A parody is merely a comical or satirical imitation of someone or something. Audiences love it when sitcom characters pay homage to celebrities or famous literary characters.

In "Lies and Dolls," a subplot parodies the *Six Million Dollar Man* series as Finch in slow motion appears to be bionic, pulling the cinder block out of the basement wall and hurling it across the room. They parody again in slow motion as Elliot escapes the police, leaping over

the toys in the toy store and running dramatically out of the store as action sequence music plays.
—*Just Shoot Me*

In "Gypsies, Tramps, and Weed," Jack parodies Cher, thinking she is really a drag queen doing a poor imitation of the actress/singer.
—*Will & Grace*

8 Physical Gags & Pratfalls

Some actors are just more agile at playing physical gags and pratfalls. If the sitcom for which you're writing has such an actor, then don't let his/her talent go to waste.

In "Baby, Part 2," Hal ends up on a back board used by paramedics. As he hallucinates from the hospital, he runs with the back board and neck brace attached, trying to race home to be there for the delivery of the baby. It makes for a great visual sight gag.
—*Malcolm in the Middle*

One of the character traits of Grace Adler is that she is clumsy. You can have fun with this by writing a lot of physical gags for her. In "And the Horse That He Rode In On…," Grace runs into a lamppost and is rescued by Leo, her future husband.
—*Will & Grace*

In "An Affair To Forget," Niles duels with his wife's fencing instructor in a hilarious bit of physical comedy.
—*Frasier*

Seinfeld's Kramer was always tripping, falling, sliding, and contorting his body for a laugh.

9 Play A Character Opposite of What's Expected

Playing a character opposite of what's expected gives you a great place to mine jokes. This comedy cone is also great for introducing new characters.

In "The Needle and the Omelet's Done," Jack's acting teacher, Zandra, is not the usual, supportive teacher. Instead, she's brutal, hostile, and bitter.

                    ZANDRA
You should bleed. You stink. You will never be
a thespian.

                    JACK
Well, duh. I'm a guy.
— *Will & Grace*

In "Big Crane On Campus," Frasier is at first charmed by an old high school classmate, Lorna, only to find out she can be a raving maniac with anger management issues.
— *Frasier*

10 Play A Visual Opposite of the Dialogue

With this comedy cone, you have a physical gag that is juxtaposed with the character's dialogue in an opposite way.

In the "Pilot" episode, Lois stands topless and exasperated as the school counselor, Caroline, tries to talk with her about Malcolm.

                    LOIS
So you're here to insult my parenting skills?

                    CAROLINE
What? No, I'm sure you're a terrific parent.

Behind Lois, we see Malcolm and Reese, wrestling on the floor in their underwear as they try to kill each other.
— *Malcolm in the Middle*

11 Potty Humor

Anything associated with bodily functions falls into this category.

In the opening tag of "If Boys Where Girls," the Wilkersons eat pizza. Lois begins telling about the babies inside the womb and placenta, keeping on until she totally grosses out her three sons who flee the table. Lois turns to Hal and smiles:

                    LOIS
        (re: the pizza)
I told you we only needed a medium.

Hal happily takes another slice of pizza.
—*Malcolm in the Middle*

In "The Needle and the Omelet's Done," Jack teaches Zandra's acting class while unknowingly Zandra watches on. Finally, she interrupts:

```
ZANDRA
Well, McFarland, I've got to say you never
disappoint. I gave you a class full of crap,
and you managed to make crap-ade.
```
—*Will & Grace*

12 Props

Use the environment. Always have a lot of props in your script, and let them play into the plot. To further use this comedy cone, use the prop in an unexpected way.

In "The One With Mac and CHEESE," Joey can't get along with his robotic co-star and nearly loses his job. In the end, he solves his problem, but as he delivers his line, the robot goes wild, trashing Joey's desk. Joey yells to the robot controller only to discover him making out with a girl and not paying attention to the controls.
—*Friends*

In "Lies and Dolls," Nina poses as a Southern Belle in order to keep dating a conservative politician, when her lie backfires. She must suddenly cook up a gourmet meal to keep up the act. Desperate for help because she knows nothing about cooking, Nina calls Maya who promises to stay on the phone with her through the whole process. Relieved, Nina follows Maya's first instructions—chop up the vegetables. She does so, and then picks up the phone again only to discover she's chopped the phone cord in half.
—*Just Shoot Me*

13 Rule of Three

Three is the magic number in comedy. When you write a gag, sometimes you'll want to times it by three; that is, repeat the gag three times.

In "The Needle and the Omelette's Done," Leo first tells Grace his parents aren't his parents. A few beats later the joke is topped by Leo

claiming the omelette chef is, then isn't his brother, and at the end of the scene the joke is played for the third time when he again says that his parents really aren't his parents.
—*Will & Grace*

In "The Canister," Ray tries to hide the canister, but is interrupted by Marie. Then he tries again, but is interrupted by Robert. Then Debra tries to hide the canister, but is interrupted by Frank. They setup a try-fail and play it three times.
—*Everybody Loves Raymond*

14 Running Gags

A running gag can run through the entire episode or through the entire series. It doesn't necessarily have to be repeated three times, but you can combine it with the above comedy cone if you like. For example:

Jack creates his own little café in the hallway outside his apartment. This little gag spins numerous jokes throughout the series.
—*Will & Grace*

Jerry and Newman polite, but full of loathing, "hello" each time they see each other.
—*Seinfeld*

Tim Taylor always creates disaster when he tries to fix something. This running gag fueled much of the shows humor.
—*Home Improvement*

15 Setup, Then Payoff

This is a gag that you set up somewhere in the episode, then pay it off before the end of the episode.

"The Marine Biologist," sets up early that George pretends to be a marine biologist and Kramer has taken up golf. We see Kramer practicing his swing at the beach, hitting the balls out to sea. Later in the episode, George walks along the beach with his girlfriend, when suddenly a whale needs help. George swims out to save it only because he doesn't want to admit that he isn't a marine biologist. At the end of the episode, George tells the group how he saved the whale—something was stuck in its blowhole. He pulls out the

obstruction—a golf ball. Kramer reacts.
—*Seinfeld*

This topper to the gag was beautifully setup as the two seemingly unrelated plots merged for a great punch line at the end.

16 Shock-Value/Surprises

Using this mechanism, you play something unexpected or randomly in the scene, or surprise the character by catching him/her off guard.

In "The Needle and the Omelette's Done," Grace is being herself and rambling on about stupid TV shows, drinking lots of champagne, and pigging out at the buffet. She is then shocked to realize she and Leo aren't just dining with old friends of Leo's, but with his parents!
—*Will & Grace*

In "The One With Ross's Wedding, Part 2," Ross flubs up. When it comes time to say, "I take thee, Emily," Ross says, "I take thee, Rachel." Ouch.
—*Friends*

One of the classic sitcom reveals ever appeared on the last episode of *Newhart*. The character turns on the light, then looks at his wife; he just had the craziest dream. His wife turns over, and surprise—it's not Joanne, but Emily, Bob's wife on *The Bob Newhart Show*, playing the second sitcom as if it had all been a dream.
—*Newhart*

17 Titles

The audience's first smile, chuckle, or laugh can come from your sitcom episode's title. By using any of the other comedy cones, you can develop a comical title for your script. Parodies and puns work well here.

"It's the Gay Pumpkin, Charlie Brown"—*Will & Grace*, "An Affair To Forget"—*Frasier*, and "Lies and Dolls"—*Just Shoot Me* (parodies)

Frasier uses title cards throughout the episode to add a humorous accent to the next segment of the show.

Likewise, *Just Shoot Me* uses the cover of Blush Magazine and its cover headlines to introduce the next segment.

18 Try-Fails

Here, a character tries and fails, then tries and fails again, over and over either throughout the episode or throughout the series. You want to keep building the gag. Each try and fail must be bigger than the one before it, and the character becomes more annoyed and/or desperate to achieve his/her goal.

In "Get Out," Michael spends the entire episode just trying and failing to get his family into the car to go to his cousin's wedding. After finally accomplishing his goal, the family exit into the garage to leave as the phone rings. Just as they drive off, a voice over is heard on the answering machine: the wedding's been called off. (That's a topper to the episode.)
—*My Wife & Kids*

In "The One Where Joey Loses His Insurance," Joey auditions, fails, auditions, fails, then auditions and finally succeeds. (Notice the magic rule of three.)
—*Friends*

NOTE: Six of the comedy cones listed above were in part derived from my first writing teacher's (Annie Montgomery) fifteen levels of humor. You'll find her six others listed under dialogue devices in Chapter Seventeen. Thanks, Annie.

Conclusion

As illustrated in the examples above, you can mix and combine comedy cones however they work for your story. The point is to fill the page with humor and play with the audience expectations as you write your gags. If you have trouble thinking up gags, classic sitcoms and/or black and white silent comedies are great sources of inspiration. "Borrow" from the best, updating the gag by giving it a new and fresh spin.

Exercise 38: Think back over the sitcoms you've watched thus far. Try to list at least one example for each comedy cone.

This exercise will help familiarize you with comedy cones to aid you as you begin writing your teleplay.

Exercise 39: With these comedy cones in mind, read back over your Teaser. Rewrite your Teaser, just focusing on the comedy and making each visual gag and joke even more clever and witty.

Exercise 40: Next, write the first two scenes of your Act One (1st and 2nd Street). Really work on creating drivers and plots the viewer (and reader) will care about and want to watch for the next half hour.

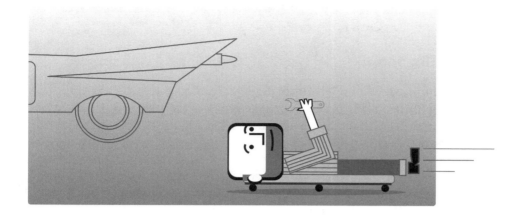

Chapter Sixteen
Joke Mechanics

One of the most important road rules of sitcom writing is:

Road Rule #16: You must create two to three jokes per page!

Sound like a lot? It is. Sitcoms thrive on jokes, and require several jokes on each and every page of your script. So it's best to utilize the plot predicament you've setup, and spin your jokes from the story and characters whenever possible. This way, the jokes and laughs flow naturally. You don't ever want to force a joke. Viewers won't grin; they'll grimace at the lazy and trite writing.

So just what exactly constitutes a great joke, you ask? Well, to paraphrase Sol Saks, writer of *The Craft of Comedy Writing*:
[A great joke = exact word + proper word placement]

Ah, but how do you choose the right words and ensure their proper placement for the biggest laughs? Simple, you just need to learn the mechanics of joke writing. So let's begin with the basics: the setup and the punch line.

The Setup

In the setup, you introduce the subject of the joke, which will be followed by the punch line that completes the joke through an unexpected twist. Whereas the setup creates the tension of the joke, the punch line releases the tension. To create a joke, you must use a setup line or a straight line on which to hang the punch line. A setup line subtly sets up the joke whereas a straight line is an ordinary line of dialogue, but one from which a punch line spin for a laugh. Look at the distinction in the following examples.

When you think setup, remember brevity: less is more in joke writing. You don't want to bury the joke in a wordy setup. The setup should be succinct. In addition, don't suggest the punch line and ruin its surprise. You must startle the viewer to get the laugh.

Your setup can comprise one line, several lines, or repeated lines. Regardless, it must include two elements: the basis of the joke (introduction to the viewer) and a beat of development, complication, or inconsistency (to create tension). If you don't have the tension, then the punch line can't release the tension and you have no joke.

In the episode "Marie's Meatballs" from *Everybody Loves Raymond,* once again, Ray's in trouble with Debra:

```
                    ROBERT
        You're in crap town, huh?
        (setup)


                    RAY
        Meet the mayor.
        (punch line)
```

Setups work well if they are logical and ordinary. With this type of setup, you'll use a straight line. The audience follows along without suspicion—then wham! Along comes the punch line. If the setup, however, feels awkward or blatant, the viewer will be waiting for the joke and your punch line arrives deflated and humorless.

In "Crazy in Love," Grace joins Will and Jack who watch basketball on TV:

> GRACE
> Have you seen Matt yet?
> (ordinary question)

> WILL
> Yeah, he's right there, right on the
> sidelines. Just four clicks left of Spike Lee.
> Just right beside that little girl and her
> grandpa.
> (logical answer)

> JACK
> Uh, that's Catherine Zeta-Jones and Michael
> Douglas.
> (punch line)
> —*Will & Grace*

One way to write subtle setups is to use everyday situations and problems that your viewer can relate to. Then, your viewer understands the stress your characters are feeling; characters are stressed, audience feels stressed, and yes, now you have tension for your punch line. By having the audience thinking, "yeah, I've been there," you've got their minds on their experience, and they won't see the punch line coming. When it does arrive, they won't know what hit them; but they will definitely appreciate the joke and you'll get a laugh.

In this episode of *Frasier,* the conversation centers around the holiday cooking, questions the audience hears every Thanksgiving in their homes:

> NILES
> How far along are you?
> (straight line)

> LILITH
> I'm nearly done defrosting.
> (setup line)

```
                    NILES
        And the turkey?
        (punch line)
        —Frasier
```

Furthermore, the setup can be placed within a conversation or a scene or a series of scenes (which really hides it and keeps the punch line a surprise).

The Punch Line

The punch line is the twist or surprise that completes the joke. It does so in an unexpected manner which is why your audience laughs.

Have you ever watched your favorite sitcom, and then shouted out the punch line before the character did? Not to downplay your genius, but in such situations, that's an example of lazy or tired sitcom writing. It means the writer went for the obvious joke and the setup was blatant because it lead you right to the joke. Don't make your punch lines predictable, or you'll lose the laugh. There's a reason it's called a "punch" line. Make sure your punch line arrives with a punch!

Using shared problems and distresses as we discussed above in the setup is one way to sneak your way into a joke, but you can also slip in by using current trends, hot topics, or cultural experiences (remember comedy cone). Viewers love these types of jokes because it makes them feel in the loop.

Drew rebels and refuses to collect the other employees' urine for drug testing (a current issue in the world of employment) so his boss demands Drew turn in a sample:

```
                    MR. WICK
        I want your pee on my desk tomorrow morning!


                    DREW
        Oh, it will be on your desk tomorrow morning.


                    MR. WICK (OS)
        In a cup.
```

```
                    DREW
    Oh, it'll be in a cup.

                    MR. WICK (OS)
    Not my coffee cup!
    —The Drew Carey Show
```

Notice how each line of dialogue builds the tension to create a strong punch line at the end.

Don't be nervous about writing jokes. Remember, you've got to build the dramatic tension of the story, the characters, and their relationships to help spark the tension in your jokes. This is a great place from which to fuel the laughs.

For example, let's look at how the relationships of the characters on *Frasier* affect their dialogue:

Niles and Martin:

```
                    MARTIN
    The disposal's jammed. You want to stick your
    hand down there and see what's stuck?
    (straight line)


                    NILES
    Dad, it's me, Niles.
    (punch line)
```

This uses the personality traits of the characters. In this case, Niles, who is obsessive about his appearance and certainly not handy around the house.

Daphne and Niles:

```
                    DAPHNE
    I suppose I like my gents more on the manly
    side.
```

She glances at the napkin Niles holds.

```
                    DAPHNE
    Oh, is that a little swan you just made
```

<pre>
                    NILES
          No, it was a B-52.
</pre>

This bit plays off the sexual tension of the couple, and the fact that Niles is hopelessly in love with Daphne and always trying to impress her, although she is unaware of his feelings at this point in the series.

Frasier and Niles:

<pre>
                   FRASIER
          Where was I?

                    NILES
          You were last seen climbing Mount Ego.
</pre>

This punch line derives from the brothers' constant rivalry.

Punch lines, for obvious reasons, must come at the end of the joke. Usually, it comes at the end of a character's dialogue block (speech). You don't want the character to keep talking after the punch line, because then he's stepping over the laugh, thus:

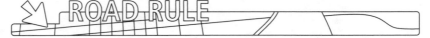

Road Rule #17: Don't go past the joke.

This doesn't mean, however, that you can't have several jokes within the same speech, it just means that if you do, you need to cue the actor to pause (by putting in parenthesis "a beat" or "…") so that the audience can absorb the first joke before the actor moves on to the second.

One last tip on punch lines: if you have a weak punch line and you truly can't improve it, then check your setup line. Most likely, that's where the fault exists. By adjusting or changing your setup, you can usually unblock your creative juices, and get the punch lines flowing again.

Types of Jokes

Below, is a list of various jokes. Mix and match them in your script to keep creating big laughs. Notice the setup lines as you read the following examples to each joke type.

- Callback Jokes
- Comebacks or One-Liners
- Monologue Jokes
- Parodies (Verbal)
- Puns
- Put-Downs
- Running Jokes
- Toppers
- Triples

1 Callback Jokes

When you refer back to a joke only once in the episode, using a joke that's already been setup and paid off in order to get an additional laugh, the second joke is known as a callback joke. This is another frugal way of writing jokes.

In "And the Horse He Rode In On," a handsome stranger on a horse rescues Grace after she runs into a lamp post. As they ride on the horse, she finally asks:

>   GRACE
> ...Why do you have a horse in Manhattan?

>   LEO
> I rented him in the park. Some weeks we ride,
> some weeks we just get a pretzel.

At the end tag of the episode, this joke is called back as Leo stands beside a pretzel vender with his horse:

>   LEO
> Two please. With mustard.

The horse snorts.

                    LEO
          Uh... one with no mustard.
          —*Will & Grace*

The joke has already been setup in the second scene of act one, and is played for a second time in the callback in the end tag of the episode.

2 Comebacks or One-Liners

A comeback is a sarcastic or humorous response by one character to another.

                    FRANK
          I tried nice once. Didn't care for it.

                    MARIE
          Is that what happened to smart?
          —*Everybody Loves Raymond*

                    CARRIE
          One woman's Titanic is another woman's Love
          Boat.
          —*Sex & the City*

                    ROBERT
          I have some exciting news!

                    FRANK
          Your blue ox came home?
          —*Everybody Loves Raymond*

3 Monologues

This is when a character gives a long speech, has a tantrum, or goes off on a tirade, monopolizing the dialogue. Monologues generally contain a beginning, middle, and end which utilize the comedic tension. Here, you can chatter or rant on without killing the joke, because the babbling or ranting is actually building the joke.

In an episode of *Sex & the City,* Miranda has fallen into a rut, using food to comfort her in her recent depression. In a low moment, she digs through the trash to eat the cake she's previously thrown out.

She then calls Carrie in a panic, leaving this message on Carrie's answering machine:

> MIRANDA
> ...I feel you need to know that your good friend, Miranda Hobbes, has just taken a piece of cake out of the garbage and eaten it. You'll probably need this information when you check me into the Betty Crocker Clinic.

Notice, the monologue builds to the punch line parodying the Betty Ford Clinic.

In this famous monologue from a *M*A*S*H* episode, Frank Burns has been left in charge of the 4077, but when Frank orders Hawkeye to comply with regulations and carry a gun, he replies:

> HAWKEYE
> ...I'll carry your books, I'll carry a torch, I'll carry a tune, I'll carry on, carry over, carry forward, Cary Grant, cash and carry, carry me back to Old Virginia, I'll even 'hari-kari' if you'll show me how, but I will not carry a gun!
> —*M*A*S*H*

Notice, it contains ordinary dialogue mixed with clichés and puns for a witty monologue.

4 Parody (Verbal)

Parodies, puns, and put-downs, oh my! They are the life blood of sitcom jokes. A verbal parody is a comical or satirical verbal imitation of someone or something.

In "Kisses Sweeter Than Wine," having a bad day, Frasier takes it out on his dad who merely asks what's happened when he sees Frasier's face:

> FRASIER
> I cut myself shaving without water. And why was there no water? Because I had to move your chair, which gouged the floor, which made me call for Joe, who found bad pipes, who called

for Cecil, who ate the cat that killed the rat
that lived in the house that Frasier built!
—*Frasier*

Notice, this parody combines with a monologue which contains a beginning, a middle, and an end which culminates in the parody.

In "The One on the Last Night" episode from *Friends,* Rachel and Monica fight:

> RACHEL
> Ooooh, I'm Monica. I wash the toilet seventeen times a day, even when people are on it!

5 Puns

Most sitcom writers love puns. A pun is just the humorous use of a word in a way that suggests two or more interpretations. Puns are funny because they lead the audience in one direction, then slam them in another direction, thus laughs ensue.

When Colonel Potter and Hawkeye are trapped in a foxhole, drunk:

> POTTER
> I said fire that weapon!
>
> HAWKEYE
>   (to gun)
> You're fired!
>
>   (to Potter)
> I did that as gently as I could.
>
> POTTER
> That was an order, Pierce.
>
> HAWKEYE
>   (snapping his fingers)
> Oh, waiter, would you take this man's order please?
> —*M*A*S*H*

In addition, by using the literal meaning of the word, you can create surprise because you lead the audience in one direction, then switch them in another direction.

In "Ain't Nobody's Business if I Do," Frasier and Niles go ballistic when they discover Martin intends to propose to Sherry.

> DAPHNE
> I've got some shocking news. I found a ring in your father's underwear drawer.

> FRASIER
> What on earth would leave a ring around his underwear drawer?!
> —*Frasier*

6 Put-Downs

A put-down is a bit like name calling, or an insult. Certain sitcoms, such as *The Drew Carey Show,* flourish by using this joke type. In one episode, Drew tells Mimi:

> DREW
> Bing...bam...boom; the sound three mirrors make when you look at them.

In "The Canister," from *Everybody Loves Raymond,* Robert informs Marie that Frank is sneaking bites from the Easter ham she's prepared. As she starts to leave, she states:

> MARIE
> Well, I should go, there's a pig eating my ham.

In "Basil the Rat," from *Fawlty Towers,* Sybil tells her husband, Basil, that her friends all think he's anti-social and weird. They can't imagine how the two of them got together:

> SYBIL
> Black magic, my mother says.

She walks into the next room. Basil mutters to himself:

```
                         BASIL
          Well, she'd know, wouldn't she. Her and that
          cat.
```

7 Running Jokes

Remember the comedy cone running gags in the previous chapter? This works great for joke writing as well. In a running joke, the same character or different characters may repeat the original punch line in a new situation, or different characters may deliver variations of the punch line, all using the original setup to pay off the newly created punch lines. Running jokes are very economical too, because you've already setup the joke, paid it off with the punch line, and then return to it a couple of times during the episode.

In the "Pilot" of *Malcolm in the Middle*, Lois repeatedly tells her sons to, "stop playing with yourself."

Running jokes can also play throughout a series. For example, the introduction bit always played between Newman and Jerry on *Seinfeld* as they loathingly said hello to each other.

8 Toppers

These are great because they are so economical. You've already setup the joke, and paid it off with a punch line. Now, you just top that punch line. If you're lucky, you might get one or two extra laughs because the joke naturally lends itself to a topper(s). Thus, from one setup and punch line, you might get three punch lines! That's frugal writing and brevity; remember those rules in joke writing. Besides, once you get the viewer chuckling at the first punch line, you're likely to get a belly laugh by the third punch line because the viewer just keeps upping his/her laughter as the jokes keep topping themselves.

In "Traffic School," Raymond is bored and annoyed at having to sit with his family and be supportive of Robert who practices his lecture on them:

```
                        ROBERT
          Now, I'd like each of you to tell us what
          offense led to you being here today?
          (setup)
```

```
                    RAY
        I killed my brother
        (punch line)


                    ROBERT
        Traffic offense, Ray.
        (straight line)


                    RAY
        With my car.
        (topper)
```
—*Everybody Loves Raymond*

Again, the magical rule of three can be applied to toppers, too. Don't top a joke more than two times or you're milking the joke too much, and viewers might feel the story has stopped just so the character can deliver jokes.

Furthermore, make sure the setup can carry the topper. You don't want to dilute a great punch line. Sometimes, the punch line should stand alone. It all depends on the context of the joke and what's happening in the story.

If you do decide to top a punch line, then the second punch line must be even wittier than the first (or at least as witty) and the third punch line, even wittier than the previous two. It's called a topper for a reason. Keep upping/topping the jokes and laughs.

9   The Triple

Remember the rule of three? Well, it applies to joke writing, too. If you have a setup, a setup, and then the punch line, this is known by comedy writers as a triple.

In "Basil the Rat" from *Fawlty Towers,* Basil tries to get his mostly Spanish-speaking bellhop, Manuel, to go up to the water tank and fish out two dead pigeons. Manuel starts laughing and "oinking" as he misinterprets Basil, thinking Basil said two pigs flew into the water tank.

```
                    BASIL
        Will you stop... pull yourself together ...Not
```

```
pigs! Pigeons!
(setup)


                    MANUEL
Que?
(setup)
```

Basil grabs a Spanish to English dictionary, searching for the word:

```
                    BASIL
Pigeon! Pigeon! Like your English! (punchline)
```

In addition, when using these popular joke types, keep in mind:

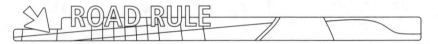

Road Rule #18: The bigger the better!

Exaggerate the joke to the 'nth degree and go for the belly laughs.

The Recap

Okay, let's review the principles discussed in this chapter:

1 Humor in dialogue must sound effortless and natural.

2 Always vary your setups, joke types, etc.… Focusing on just one-liners gets tiresome and makes your script a bland read. Spice it up!

3 By using one setup to play several jokes, you can easily meet your sitcom joke page quota, while continuing plots and layering characters.

4 Remember, every syllable and every word give a rhythm to the joke. Too many words and your joke will be diluted to the point of being humorless.

   NOTE: If you're debating on whether or not a word is working, or that you have too many words cluttering the joke, than it probably isn't working and you probably do have too many words.

5 Likewise, too few words and the viewer (and actor) might miss the joke completely.

It's a delicate balance that takes practice, practice, practice. Don't worry about making each joke perfect as you get it on the page, just get the jokes flowing. Sitcom writing is 15% first draft, 35% rewriting, and 50% polishing. Get used to it. If you go on staff, you'll spend at least half of your time polishing and fine-tuning jokes and gags.

Study the sitcom for which you are writing. Follow its lead on what's acceptable for jokes and humor on that particular sitcom.

Exercise 41: Select a general topic, or a subject taken from the headlines, or a current issue. Write a dozen factual statements or word associations about this subject. Don't try to be comical here: as Joe Friday said, "Just the facts." Next, use the list to form a setup and punch line, or just go straight for the punch line. For example:

Let's say we pick the general topic of insurance. First, let's list some facts or words we associate with insurance.

1. Double indemnity

2. Life, car, home, renters insurance

3. Cause of death

4. Need death certificate for life insurance claims

5. Premiums

6. Accidental

7. Act of God

8. Insurance salesman

9. Most people hate dealing with insurance

10. Claims department

11. Approved claims

12. Claims denied

From this list, you might come up with a joke such the one below:

In "Chuckles Bites the Dust" from *The Mary Tyler Moore Show*, Murray and Lou discuss the tragic death of Chuckles the Clown, who, while dressed as Peter Peanut and marching in a parade, is shelled to death by a "rogue elephant":

```
                    MURRAY
         Can you imagine the insurance claim? Cause of
         Death: A busted goober.
```

With this situation, you can imagine the jokes that spawned naturally from the humor of the ridiculous circumstance surrounding the clown's death. Perhaps, that's why this episode is quoted as being one of the best ever written.

Exercise 42: Now write the rest of your Act One (3rd—10th Streets). Once you've finished this exercise, you should have your first 19–22 pages, depending upon your story.

Exercise 43: Choose a scene from your Act One and rewrite the jokes using the principles and techniques discussed in this chapter. Make a list as you did in exercise 41 to get your brainwaves activated if you get stuck on certain jokes.

Chapter Seventeen
Sitcom Dialogue

Dialogue in sitcoms is extremely difficult to write because in addition to hiding exposition (important plot information) and capturing a character's speech rhythms and patterns, the sitcom writer must also be continually setting up jokes and delivering jokes on every page of the script! And while juggling all of this, the writer must also remember:

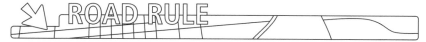

Road Rule #19: Arrive late and leave early in dialogue.

You've got to zoom into the dialogue as fast as you can, keep the story moving, and keep the audience laughing.

Dialogue Sitcom Style

The type and style of dialogue you use in your episode will mainly depend on these four factors:

- The Character's Compass Traits and Dipsticks
- The Characters' Relationships
- The Comedic Tone

• The Network or Cable Station It Airs On

Let's look at how these factors affect a sitcom's dialogue.

1 The Character's Compass Traits and Dipsticks

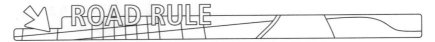

Road Rule #20: Don't take your audience out of the script by using dialogue uncharacteristic to the character!

A character's traits and dipstick data will definitely affect their dialogue. Obviously, if a character is an adult, he/she will speak differently than a toddler. An Australian, British, or Russian character will have vocabulary unique to each one's own country. For example, a British person will refer to his apartment as a flat, to cigarettes as "ciggies" or "fags." They go "on holidays" or "to hospital" (dropping the article in each) instead of saying they are going "on a holiday" or "to the hospital." Likewise, a character from New Jersey will speak differently than one from Mississippi. Let the character's personality traits and history play into the dialogue.

> DAPHNE
> I'm from England, the country that used to own you people.
> —*Frasier*

Klinger was always in drag, hoping to get a Section 8. See how his character's quirkiness impacts Dr. Freedman's dialogue as he speaks to Klinger:

> SIDNEY
> You're a tribute to man's endurance. A monument of hope in size twelve pumps. I hope you do get out someday. There would be a battalion of men in hoop skirts right behind you.
> —*M*A*S*H*

In addition, a character's race, culture, social status, and occupation also influence his/her dialogue. A doctor will speak differently than a waitress, cop, or a lawyer, as each will have their respective occupational jargon and education to factor into the dialogue equation. These factors give diversity to the characters' vocabulary and flavor the dialogue. Use these factors to sharpen the dialogue.

Notice the vocabulary Niles, a psychiatrist, uses, and how the writer's play with the character relationships of Niles and his father, Martin, an ex-cop.

```
                    NILES
     He's clearly the one dealing with repressed
     material, not to mention the obvious Oedipal
     issues.


                    MARTIN
     Argle, garle, gobble, goop.


                    NILES
     What?


                    MARTIN
     Now you know how it feels. What are you
     talking about?
     —Frasier
```

2 The Character's Relationships

The relationship between characters always dictates dialogue style. Conversation is a two-way street. In addition, many characters that are siblings, spouses, and/or close friends, will have a certain shorthand or dialogue rhythm with each other that you'll have to learn or create when writing for such characters.

For example, in *Will & Grace*, they often finish each other sentences. When they play charades, they always win because just one little mannerism and the other one gets the clue. It's a shorthand humor that only they usually understand, leaving everyone else flabbergasted. They finish each other's sentences like an old married couple. This shorthand is often acknowledged by the characters and played for additional laughs:

Will and Grace argue: she wants him to join her in doing something for charity since she prayed for concert tickets as he dialed in to be the 105th caller.

```
                    GRACE
      We can argue this out or we can just
      shorthand it.


                    WILL
      Shorthand.


                    GRACE
      Will, do it.


                    WILL
      No.


                    GRACE
      Yes.


                    WILL
      Okay.
```
—*Will & Grace*

Thus, as you start writing your characters, remember their back story and the relationships they have with the characters around them so you can enrich their dialogue.

3 The Comedic Tone

Does farce, satirical, or cerebral comedy dominate the series? This will make a huge difference in the type of jokes and dialogue the characters will be speaking.

You won't find witty and intellectual sparring on *Married With Children*, but you will hear such dialogue on *Frasier*.

Scrubs dialogue will be speckled with medical jargon while *Spin City* dialogue tosses around political vernacular. Likewise, if you're writing a historical piece, then time and place will affect your dialogue. The characters in *That 70's Show* can't be talking about DVD's and mobile phones that take pictures.

4 The Network or Cable Station It Airs On

The audience the network or cable channel aims for will greatly influence a sitcom's dialogue. Each network or cable station has its own set of rules and standards that it goes by. These standards will also affect your dialogue. The major networks such as ABC, NBC, CBS, and FOX (although FOX is a little edgier) are more conservative in the language and subject matter that they allow to be aired; whereas cable channels such as HBO and Showtime can air more adult language and content. Warner Bros. strives for the teen and family audience and PAX targets the whole family so their series reflect fairly clean (no obscenities) dialogue. Thus, if you're writing dialogue for *Reba,* your characters better not sound like Samantha Jones on *Sex & the City*.

Watch and really listen to the sitcom for which you want to write. See what is acceptable and consistent to that sitcom. If writing an original pilot, study the various sitcoms produced by a specific network and/or studio so you can get a really good idea of what's acceptable and preferable to them. This will give you a guideline of what to do in your own dialogue as well as where to try to sell your script.

After considering these factors when writing, what's next? Learning to write brilliant and hysterical sitcom dialogue.

Sitcom Dialogue Devices

These devices can make your script dialogue read more fascinating and/or funnier. Mix and match as often as you can.

- Act Out Lines
- Alliterations
- Character Asks A Question
- Character Asks and Answers His/Her Own Question
- Character Answers With A Question
- Character Defends Him/Herself
- Character Gives Advice
- Character Gives Order

- Character Makes An Exclamation
- Characters Makes An Observation
- Character Misinterprets Conversation
- Character Misinterprets Scene
- Clichés
- Complaints
- Interrupt Character
- Interrupt Scene
- Narrators
- Quotes
- Repeating Dialogue
- Signature Lines
- Threats/Ultimatums
- Words Which Sound Funny

1 Act Out Lines

This is the last line of dialogue in an act, teaser, or tag. It usually gives the viewer a laugh before the commercial break and/or acts as a sitcom cliffhanger:

At the end of Act One, Malcolm reluctantly rides with his pregnant mother to his aunt's house; a long, three hour drive. Lois has been concerned about Malcolm's attentiveness to his girlfriend. So now that she has him "hostage," she tells Malcolm she's glad they have some quality time together, but Malcolm's bored:

```
                    MALCOLM
        What are we gonna talk about for three hours?


                    LOIS
        Sex.
```

Malcolm reacts horrified, and tries to escape the car.
—*Malcolm in the Middle*

2 Alliterations

Simple phonetics bring a smile. By putting together a string of words with the same initial sounds, you create a phonetic rhythm in the phase that just naturally sounds funny.

Colonel Potter arrives to a camp full of lunatics. Klinger rushes to introduce himself, in full drag, of course. He salutes:

```
             KLINGER
Colonel Potter, sir, Corporal Klinger. I'm
Section Eight head to toe. I'm wearing a
Warner bra…. I like to play with dolls. My
last wish is to be buried in my mother's
wedding gown. I'm nuts. I should be out.


          COLONEL POTTER
Horse-hockey!
```
—*M*A*S*H*

Colonel Potter often used alliterations in his exclamations (say that fast three times). Horse-hockey, buffalo bagels,…

3 Character Asks A Question

Here, you build the lines and/or jokes off a question.

Rachel and Monica check out the new eye doctor:

```
             MONICA
Oh, my God! How cute is the new eye doctor?


             RACHEL
So cute I'm thinking about jamming this pen
in my eye.
```
—*Friends*

As George and Jerry get ready to go get some dinner, they debate on where to eat. Jerry suggests eating Chinese again, but George complains they ate Chinese last night:

```
             GEORGE
Who eats Chinese food two nights in a row?
```

> JERRY
> About two billion Chinese people.
> —*Seinfeld*

4 Character Asks and Answers His/Her Own Question

With this device, the character asks a question, then answers it before anyone else can. In this way, the character is in essence setting up and paying off his/her own joke.

> DREW
> Oh, you hate your job? Why didn't you say so? There's a support group for that. It's called EVERYBODY, and they meet at the bar!
> —*The Drew Carey Show*

5 Characters Answers With A Question

Here, you build your conflict and/or humor from the character's response, using a question.

> LOIS
> You put the baby in the closet?

> HAL
> You left the milk on the table?
> —*Malcolm in the Middle*

George yearns to make a difference, well, in that George Castanza kind of way:

> GEORGE
> I really want to leave my mark this time. Like remember the summer at Dairy Queen when I cooled my feet in the soft serve?

> JERRY
> So you want to go out in a final blaze of incompetence?

> GEORGE
> Flame on!
> —*Seinfeld*

6 Character Defends Him/Herself

Here, a character defends his/her ideas, beliefs, and/or actions.

>   NILES
> Frasier, do you remember the time the Kreizel
> brothers tied me to their Great Dane and
> lobbed meatballs down their gravel driveway?

>   FRASIER
> I told you, Niles, I would have helped you,
> but their sister was holding me down.
> —*Frasier*

7 Character Gives Advice

With this device, one character counsels another. It can be serious advice or humorous advice.

After Hawkeye loses a patient, Henry tries to help him accept their jobs as surgeons in a M*A*S*H unit:

>   HENRY
> Look, all I know is what they taught me at
> command school. There are certain rules about
> a war and rule number one is young men die.
> And rule number two is doctors can't change
> rule number one.
> —*M*A*S*H*

The group has just seen Joey perform on stage as a king, and are now scanning the early editions of the newspapers for his review. As they look through the paper, Phoebe offers some advice:

>   PHOEBE
> You know, you might want to wear underwear
> next time because when you sat down we could
> see your... royal subjects.
> —*Friends*

8 Character Gives Order

As Hyde and Kelso fight over Jackie, Fez becomes impatient; after all, they're on top of the water tower supposed to be spray painting it for their last high school prank:

FEZ
Stop it! You two need to grow up and start
painting genitals on the water tower!
—*That 70's Show*

9 Character Makes Exclamation

Charlotte is horrified when she sees the tacky floral arrangement she ordered by phone at Miranda's mother's funeral. Referring to the flowers, she whispers to Carrie:

CHARLOTTE
They were suppose to say, "I'm sorry, I love
you," not, "You're dead, let's disco!"
—*Sex & the City*

10 Character Makes Observation

True to character, in their own non-sensical way, Frank makes an observation as he and Hot Lips spend some quality time together:

FRANK
Funny thing war: never have so many suffered
so much so so few could be so happy.

HOT LIPS
We're lucky to be two of the few and not the
many.

FRANK
I know, darling, and I love being both of us.
—*M*A*S*H*

11 Character Misinterprets Conversation

In this situation, two characters have a conversation in which one character is speaking on one topic and the other character is speaking on a completely different topic, yet neither realize it.

As the Wilkerson's flee the shopping mall before they are arrested, a very pregnant Lois has flashes of what her life would have been like if she had given birth to four girls instead of four boys. In her fantasy, she realizes girls are just as horrible to raise as boys. Her husband,

Hal, oblivious to her thoughts, just wants to get out of the mall. He encourages her to keep running:

```
                      HAL

     You can do it! It's only three hundred yards
     to Senor Jellybeans!
```

Lois looks at her husband in despair, referring to her epiphany. It won't matter if the baby's a boy or girl because:

```
                     LOIS
     Trust me, Hal! There's no escape! There's no
     escape, there's no escape no matter what!
```

He keeps running, not understanding what she's talking about.
—*Malcolm in the Middle*

Notice the rule of three as she repeats the line "there's no escape" three times.

You can also use this device not only to add humor, but to further your plot and build tension as the audience awaits the misinterpretation to be realized.

12 Character Misinterprets Scene

Here, a character misunderstands what is going on in the scene.

Karen flashes her breasts at another woman after she thinks the woman has just flashed her:

```
                     GRACE
     Karen, what are you doing?!


                     KAREN
     She started it!


                     GRACE
     Karen, she's breast feeding.


                     KAREN
     Oh...That would explain the little bald man.
```
—*Will & Grace*

13 Clichés

Clichés are phrases which we have heard so much they have become trite. But in television, you can have a lot of fun with them if you just spin them in an unexpected direction.

Obsessed with finding out how his teenage daughter, Claire, outsmarted him and didn't get caught at a party Michael just knew she was sneaking off to, Michael interrogates his not so smart son, Junior, trying to find out if Junior tipped Claire off:

>   MICHAEL
>   Don't play dumb with me, kid!
>
>   JUNIOR
>   I'm not playing!
>
>   MICHAEL
>   I can't argue with that.
>   —*My Wife & Kids*

Hawkeye often spun a cliché for a laugh.

>   HAWKEYE
>   It's the least I could do. I always do the
>   least I can do.
>   —*M*A*S*H*

14 Complaints

Here, a character makes a criticism or objection to someone.

Unable to face one more day of fish and liver in the cafeteria, Hawkeye rants:

>   HAWKEYE
>   I've eaten a river of liver and an ocean of
>   fish. I've eaten so much fish, I'm ready to
>   grow gills. I've eaten so much liver, I can
>   only make love if I'm smothered in bacon and
>   onions!
>   —*M*A*S*H*

Often, a complaint will come as a disparaging remark from a character which can create affection/empathy for the character. In one of the most famous sitcom disparages:

```
                    RHODA
    I don't know why I should even bother to eat
    this. I should just apply it directly to my
    hips.
    —The Mary Tyler Moore Show
```

15 Interrupt the Character

Using this comedy cone, something or someone interrupts the character.

Jerry is upset when a friend converts to Judaism, and then proceeds to tell religiously incorrect jokes. He decides to discuss this with a priest and so slips into a confessional.

```
                    PRIEST
    And this offends you as a Jew?


                    JERRY
    No, it offends me as a comedian.
```

George interrupts them, poking his head into the confessional.

```
                    GEORGE
    ...Jerry, I got to talk to you.
    —Seinfeld
```

16 Interrupt the Scene

Here something or someone interrupts the scene.

Lois feels the baby kick suddenly as she's chatting with her son and daughter-in-law.

```
                    LOIS
    Wow, it's as if something upset the baby-

    (gasps)
```

Glaring with her face pressed against the window, Grandma Ida shouts through the glass:

GRANDMA IDA
Are you gonna open the door or should I lay
down in the grass and feed the worms.
—*Malcolm in the Middle*

17 Narrator

Onscreen narration is when a character's voice over (VO) is heard over various visuals. The character may or may not be in the scene as he/she talks. If he/she is in the scene, he/she isn't speaking the words we are hearing through (VO). This dialogue device can set a tone, give us insight into the character, and reveal exposition.

Narration can play throughout the episode or serve as book ends (used only at the beginning and the end of the episode). Regardless, you will type "VO" which stands for "voice over" or "OS" for off screen" after the character's name. For example, as Carrie sits typing on her computer for her column, we hear her voice over as we see the words she is typing on her computer screen:

CARRIE (VO)
...Maybe the past is like an anchor holding us
back. Maybe you have to let go of who you
were to become who you will be...
—*Sex & the City*

Another great way to use narration is with flashbacks to reveal exposition. By flashing back, the audience gets to experience the emotion and/or humor of the scene, rather than just the telling of it.

Parodying also combines well with this device. In addition, juxtaposing the narrator's dialogue with the visuals can add humor, especially when you write the opposite of what an audience expects.

18 Quotes

On sitcoms, characters often quote from great works of literature and popular films.

When a poisoned piece of veal gets mixed in with the other veal cutlets, Basil thinks he's just served the toxic veal to the health inspector as the cook asks how the cat is doing since he saw the cat nibbling off the same piece they just gave to the health inspector:

<pre>
                    BASIL
"…How's the cat? We're just about to take the
life of a Public Health Inspector, and you
want to know, 'how's the cat?' It's "gone to
London to see the Queen."
</pre>
—*Fawlty Towers*

19 Repeating Dialogue

You can repeat a line of dialogue either in the same scene or throughout the story, using it to payoff somewhere in the script. Often, it's repeated three times because in comedy, three is the magic number.

Grace tries to keep Will from discovering that she knows what her surprise birthday gift is:

<pre>
                    GRACE
I ran into Leo. But you can't tell Will I
found out. I mean, I know, but he doesn't know
I know. And now that you know I know, you
can't let Will know that you know I know, you
know?

                    JACK
No… do you know?

                    KAREN
I think I know, but I'm sure I don't care.
</pre>
—*Will & Grace*

20 Signature Lines

Sometimes, a character will use a certain catch phrase which, when used repeatedly by only that character, comes to be known as a "signature" line. When an audience hears this line, they immediately think of that particular character. If it's successful, it becomes part of our language.

Seinfeld gave us the famous line:

<pre>
               SOUP NAZI
NO SOUP FOR YOU!
</pre>

Everybody Loves Raymond brought this signature line:

> FRANK
>
> Holy Crap!

Seinfeld gave us:

> NEWMAN
>
> Hello, Jerry.
>
> JERRY
>
> Hello, Newman.

21 Threats/Ultimatums

While in drama, threats and/or ultimatums are used to heighten suspense; in sitcoms, they are used to create jokes.

Lewis gets Drew to try his burger.

> DREW
>
> Say, this burger isn't bad.
>
> LEWIS
>
> It was created in a test kitchen.
>
> DREW
>
> Test kitchen?
>
> LEWIS
>
> Oh, I'll need to ask you a few questions. Are you experiencing any side effects?
>
> DREW
>
> You're going to be experiencing some side effects if you don't tell me what's in this burger!
>
> LEWIS
>
> Mood swings, that's obvious.
> —*The Drew Carey Show*

Lois hears a crash in the next room, she goes to see what happened, but her pregnant belly is so huge, her youngest son, Dewey hides under it, holding two halves of a crystal vase he's just broken.

>   LOIS
>   No matter where you are or what you've done,
>   I'll find out!
>   —*Malcolm in the Middle*

22 Words Which Sound Funny

You can also get humor from using words which sound funny together:

Phoebe gets frustrated with Chandler about calling a girl:

>   PHOEBE
>   Stop being so testosterony!
>
>   CHANDLER
>   The real San Francisco treat.
>   —*Friends*

Jack often likes to create his own vocabulary, which a writer can have a lot of fun with:

>   JACK
>   Now you're talkin' Jackanese!
>   —*Will & Grace*

Conclusion

As illustrated from these examples, you can combine dialogue devices to strengthen dramatic conflict and/or build humor in your dialogue. Get familiar with spotting these devices as you study dialogue. It takes time and experience to learn to write dialogue well. By applying these devices, you can make your script an enjoyable and hysterical read.

Dialogue Signposts

To test your dialogue as you write, check it against these signposts:

1. Is it revealing back story, information on, or the personality of a character?

2. Is it giving the viewer more information in your plots?

3. Does it have to be said in dialogue, or would it play better to show rather than tell?

4. Is the line of dialogue really necessary, or can it be eliminated altogether?

5. If it's a joke, is it funny?

Examine each line, especially the first and last lines of dialogue in a scene. Can you cut them and zoom right into the scene? Most likely, you can. Just because television allows you more time with dialogue, doesn't mean that you want to waste a line with inconsequential chatter. Unless of course, that is the style of a particular character, and you're playing it for humor.

Exercise 44: Pick a scene from your script with the longest amount of dialogue that you've already written. Go through this scene, reviewing ONLY the dialogue. Rewrite it using any of the dialogue devices to make your dialogue wittier.

Exercise 45: Next, go back through the same scene, and rewrite the dialogue again. This time apply Road Rule #19: Arrive late and leave early in your dialogue. Use the dialogue signposts. If any piece of dialogue does not correctly follow them, dump it! It's littering your page. Once you've rewritten the dialogue, reread your scene. Listen to how much tighter it sounds and how your pacing has improved.

NOTE: Don't worry about making your dialogue perfect—just familiarize yourself with these dialogue devices as you focus on getting the plot and characters onto the page. Don't start rewriting Act One yet, just this one scene. The rewrite comes in a later chapter.

Exercise 46: Choose several ordinary items from your household. They can be food items, office supplies, toiletries, whatever. Then, combine two or more of these items to create your own cartoon. Think of the items as if they were drawn or photographed and in a magazine: what would the caption read? Create at least 10 different combinations from the items, then list several captions for each one. For example:

Let's say you choose two melons as your items. One melon is solid, pale green while the other melon is light green with dark horizontal stripes. The caption for this combination might show the striped melon stating: "Sweetheart, do these stripes make me look fat?" Just have fun with it.

Exercise 47: Write the opening of your Act Two (11th Street). Make sure to make your U-Turn strong and witty. Include the dialogue devices discussed in this chapter.

Chapter Eighteen
Prose: Your Information Highway

All the words on your page that aren't dialogue or sluglines (which are always in CAPS and underlined in sitcoms) make up your prose. It's the words you use in describing your scene or the action of your scene; the information you give to the reader.

In sitcom format, the prose will always be in CAPS just like the slugline, and single spaced if the show is filmed before a live audience, as in *Everybody Loves Raymond* or *Will & Grace*. If the setting is already established, then you don't have to describe it; if the setting is new, then you do.

In addition, always list all the characters who are or who will be in the scene in parenthesis. Furthermore, anytime a character enters, exits, or moves around in a scene, underline it. This helps the actor when practicing run-throughs (reading through the script as they get the staging and lines down and as the writers/producers can get a feel for how the jokes sound).

For example, the format for in "Sweet & Sour Charity," *Will & Grace* would look like this:

```
INT. KAREN'S APARTMENT—DAY                    (slugline)
(KAREN, JACK, ROSARIO)                        (actors in scene)


JACK FOLLOWS KAREN INTO HER ENORMOUS AND ORDERLY
CLOSET –                                       (prose)



                    JACK

      (GASPS) If my closet looked like this, I'd

      never have come out.
```

NOTE: Later in the scene Rosario would appear since she is listed in the parenthesis above. Also notice that the dialogue is doubled spaced. In our previous chapters the dialogue examples are single spaced;

this is just to save space (and a few trees). Follow the example above in formatting your script. Sitcom dialogue is always double spaced for the actors if the show films or tapes before a live audience. It's only single spaced if the series is filmed without a live audience, like *Malcolm in the Middle*.

NOTE: In addition, if the series is video taped before a live audience, like on some cable series with lower budgets, then the prose is double spaced just like the dialogue. You'll just have to obtain copies of scripts from the series for which you're writing to know their exact format (see the addresses listed in the last chapter for places to find such scripts).

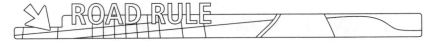

Road Rule #21: Less is more! Especially in sitcom prose.

In the example above, see how economical the prose is? Don't drown the reader or the actor with excess prose. Give the actor whatever direction he/she needs, and whatever else is necessary for the setup, then jump into the dialogue ASAP. Sitcoms are talky because they're all about the jokes. Whatever's written in the prose won't be heard by the audience, so you don't have to flower it up as you do when writing one-hour episodes or feature films. Just get the actor into the dialogue and jokes as fast as you can.

NOTE: If writing an original pilot, you will be introducing more, so it's okay to be a little more stylish. You don't have to use the "Just the facts" sparseness that you want to strive for when writing for an existing show, but do be succinct.

There are two other important factors to consider when writing prose:

1. Choose action verbs over linking verbs. Use strong and interesting word choices in your prose.

2. Eliminate excess words. Don't describe every bit of action, only what's necessary.

For example, in your prose:

Don't write:

DEBRA IS CLEANING A VERY MESSY KITCHEN, AND IS
ANNOYED BY RAY WHO JUST SITS AT THE KITCHEN TABLE
READING THE NEWSPAPER AND NOT HELPING HER.
(26 words)

Write:

DEBRA SLAMS POTS INTO THE SINK, CUING RAY HE BETTER
GET HIS BUTT OUT OF THAT CHAIR AND HELP.
(19 words)

See how the second example uses stronger action words as well as captures the tone of *Everybody Loves Raymond* and the traits of the characters. By using better word choices, it also eliminates seven words and makes the prose lean.

Also in your prose, you can direct the rhythm of the scene to indicate a pause before a character responds or the action resumes. In the example below, you might want the character of Grace to pause so Jack's punch line is absorbed before she bursts into laughter. Thus, you would write:

GRACE ABSORBS JACK'S STATEMENT. A BEAT. SHE BURSTS
INTO LAUGHTER.

"A beat" is a common term to cue the actor and/or director that a dramatic or comedic pause is needed. It's punctuation for the scene. But don't overuse; it's a bit like using an exclamation mark in your writing. Do so sparingly so it stands out for the effect that you want.

Exercise 48: Pick a scene that you've already written, one that is heavy on prose. Go through the scene, eliminating excess words and using strong action verbs. Make sure your word choices read well. Now reread it. Notice how much smoother it reads.

Exercise 49: Now finish writing your Act Two (12th-20th Streets). This Act should consist of about 18–22 pages, too. Keep your driver on course, keep escalating the plot(s) and zoom the plot(s) into the climax with much hilarity. Once you complete this exercise, you should have somewhere between 37–45 pages.

Congratulations! You just finished writing your first sitcom sample or pilot script!

Chapter Nineteen
The Scene

A scene is one of the story elements used to write a script. You create a new scene each time you switch location (even if the next scene is just in the next room) or time of day (even if the next scene is just a few minutes later). In sitcoms, the plot usually takes place over a day, or a few days at the most. This is to keep the dramatic tension of the plot from being diluted.

The length of a scene in sitcoms may vary from 1–9 pages. Most of your scenes, however, will probably range from 2–4 pages. Too long a scene and fidgety viewers might channel surf, so keep your scenes and story moving forward. In regard to format, at the beginning of each and every scene, type in the center the act number and then the scene letter (which is denoted alphabetically) skipping a space between the two. Always underline and put in CAPS. For example:

<u>ACT ONE</u>

<u>SCENE D</u>

<u>INT. BECKER'S OFFICE—DAY</u>

Scene Construction

Just as in the overall plot, each scene has a beginning, middle, and end. Likewise, scenes also need a rising incline (jeopardy) which grows steeper in each individual street (scene). Let's examine some scenes from our graphs:

In *Everybody Loves Raymond,* "The Canister," on 11th Street, Ray and Ally play video games as Debra carries a pot of mashed potatoes. She calls up to the twins (beginning of scene).

They start to leave as the twins come down the stairs. Suddenly, the canister tumbles down the stairs and lands in front of them. Ray and Debra gasp. (middle of scene: incline rising).

The Twins admit they found it in the trash while hunting Easter eggs. Debra panics; they have to sneak it back into Marie's house. Ray doesn't want to, but he'd rather risk it then face saying no to his wife. (end of scene: incline peaked).

In *Friends*, "The One Where Joey Loses His Insurance," on 4th Street, Joey visits his agent, Estelle. She yells at him for leaving her after she got him so much work. Joey tells her he didn't leave her, just hasn't been working. (beginning of scene).

Joey tells Estelle that he needs an acting job now—his SAG insurance has lapsed. Estelle says someone's been badmouthing him around town. Joey's upset, not realizing Estelle's the culprit. (middle of scene: incline rising).

Agent agrees to repair his reputation and find him work. Joey's relieved. (end of scene: incline peaked).

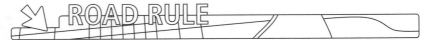

As you construct your plot, keep in mind:

Road Rule #22: Arrive late and leave early in your scenes.

Just as in your dialogue, you want to enter a scene at the last possible second and leave as soon as you possibly can. In addition, it's important to remember:

Road Rule #23: Your character must leave each scene needing more and/or knowing more than when he/she entered it!

In our examples above, this road rule plays out like this:

On 11th Street, Debra and Ray learn the canister was not thrown out. They need to get rid of it or confess. Debra insists they sneak it back into Marie's house.
—*Everybody Loves Raymond*

On 4th Street, Joey learns that Estelle was mad at him and his reputation's been tarnished around town. Estelle now knows that she needs to repair Joey's reputation and get him on auditions.
—*Friends*

As you construct your scenes, think about them in terms of telling their own mini-story. When your character enters the scene you are writing, that's the most important scene to him/her. Your characters don't know what is coming next, so don't write as if they do. This is what helps build the tension and create the humor.

Slippery When Wet—The Oblique Scene

So what makes a scene unique? Keep in mind that whatever you think of first is what every other writer's going to think of, too. Really dig deep for ideas. Think of at least three to five ways to approach the same scene, then discard the first three because by your fourth or fifth attempt, you've probably come up with something fresh.

Road Rule #24: Write the unexpected scene. Keep surprising the viewer (and the characters) in a comical manner.

Forget the obvious and write the oblique scene by sliding your driver in an unexpected direction, especially when writing a comical scene, because it is the unexpected that tickles our funny bone and makes us laugh.

The best way to achieve writing a unique scene is to take a scene that is familiar to an audience and put a spin on it; slide it in a direction they aren't expecting. When you watch TV, pay attention to what scenes catch you unexpectedly, and what scenes bring a surprise laugh. Take note, because this is what you want to do in your own scripts to create comedy, suspense, and drama.

In *Everybody Loves Raymond*, "The Canister," we see a typical scene at Easter time, a child and a parent coloring Easter eggs, in the teaser.

But the scene is slid into a funny direction as Ray competes with his six-year-old as Marie compliments Ally on her decorating skills.

In *Friends,* "The One Where Joey Loses His Insurance," Chandler enters the apartment, a typical everyday occurrence. Yet the scene slips in another direction as Chandler sees Joey writhing in pain on the floor. He's just injured himself, and now has a huge hernia popping out of his abdomen.

As mentioned before, *Newhart* really ended its series with a fabulous topper. Dick Loudon, or so we think, awakes in the middle of the night. He flips on the light and states that he just had a really crazy dream. His wife turns over to ask about the dream. The viewer is expecting to see Joanna, but instead, it's Emily (played by Suzanna Pleshette). Thus, now the viewer realizes that the whole *Newhart* series was just a dream. It's really Bob and Emily in their apartment in Chicago from the original *Bob Newhart Show.* That's great sitcom writing!

Push yourself to write original, clever, and memorable scenes. Every street and beat must keep the viewer riding along with your characters. Be creative; keep the viewers guessing where the story and the scene are going. Make your driver smash into a scene head-on by hurling something emotional or unexpected at him. Your job as a sitcom writer is to make your driver's life difficult for those 37–45 pages. Take that job seriously and comically.

Remember, it's not rocket science here. It's just taking the everyday small stuff, filling it with surprises, and exaggerating everything to the nth degree. Of course, you must do this in a hilarious manner— that's the tricky part.

Exercise 50: Choose the longest scene you've written, and rewrite it from three different approaches using the three Road Rules in this chapter. Number each attempt. Don't edit any of your ideas as you write, just write whatever comes to mind.

Once you've written these three different versions take a one week Pit Stop. Do not proceed to Exercise 52 until you have "tuned-up" your imagination with the next exercise. You must approach your work with fresh eyes.

Exercise 51: Collect a series of 15 cartoons from newspapers or magazines, ones that made you smile or chuckle. Now rewrite the captions. Try to think up several new captions per cartoon. Keep improving on the caption to see if you can come up with a better line than the original. Then, write the original caption on a list with your own captions. Show the cartoons to friends and see which captions get the best laughs.

The exercise above will help keep you thinking in terms of jokes/gags, both visual and verbal. It will also help you think economically as captions require frugality of words.

Exercise 52: Okay, now that you've had a week to clear your mind, read your scene attempts from Exercise 50 along with your original scene. Which one reads the best? Which version sounds the freshest and most interesting? It won't be your first attempt. Insert the scene you like best into your script before moving to the next chapter.

Chapter Twenty
The Rewrite

Now that you've got your script written, it's time to clean up your streets. This is where the real work begins. As you go through the exercises in this chapter, keep in mind: there are plenty of writers who will make sure their script has flawless plots, fully layered characters, unique scenes, great dialogue, and hysterical jokes. They put in the extra hours, rewriting and polishing their scripts. These writers are your competition so:

Road Rule #25: Rewrite! Rewrite! Rewrite!

You want to drive through your script using the checklists below. Drive through only one checklist at a time. DO NOT attempt to check your scripts scene by scene using all the checklists at once. You need to approach it from an overall view, and then move inward. Take appropriate Pit Stops between each "drive" through your script. Don't start a new pass when you're tired of your script (and you will get tired of it—that's when you know to take a Pit Stop).

Structure Checklist

If you diligently structured your Sitcom Road Map, your plot should be on track, but it's smart to make sure your characters didn't drive off the road as you were writing. Fix any crumbling streets in this first rewrite.

Exercise 53: Go through your script using the checklist below, and scrutinize your structure. Examine only your plots.

1. If any two scenes accomplish exactly the same thing, cut one. No matter how brilliant it may be—lose it!

2. Does your Teaser truly hook the viewer (or reader) in the first few pages?

3. Have you written your scenes so each city block has its own incline (jeopardy or what's at stake) which is rising? Does your city block also increase each plots speed (tension)?

4. Have you created enough falling rocks for your characters within each city block?

5. Are your Green Light and U-Turn strong enough to speed your story toward the climax?

6. Is the predicament you've created funny enough to sustain the humor and the plot(s) for Two Acts?

Character Checklist

Now that you have passed through your script and inspected it for structure, do the same with your characters.

Exercise 54: Using the checklist below, examine your characters and ONLY your characters.

1. Have you setup from whose POV the story will be about for the episode?

2. Is your driver(s) consistent to his/her world, dipstick, true north, and character compass?

3. Are your supporting characters and antagonist, if applicable, also consistent?

4. Are your characters unique, fun, and interesting? Are they relatable to your audience?

5. When you first introduced your characters, did you make their character tags memorable?

6. Have you created a strong enough goal and emotional need for your character that plays to the humor?

7. Have you created a worthy adversary for your driver, if applicable? Does your antagonist have a forceful goal and emotional need which is in direct conflict of your driver's goal and/or need?

Scene Checklist

Do not proceed unless you've taken a few days off.

Exercise 55: With the checklist below, evaluate your script scene by scene.

1. Does each scene have its own beginning, middle, and end? Is it building as well?

---

2. Have you written the unexpected scene or a scene the audience has experienced many times?

3. Is your character leaving each scene, knowing and/or needing more than when he/she entered it?

4. Do you arrive late and leave early in each of your scenes, or can you jump in faster and/or exit more quickly?

5. Have you hooked your viewer for the next week's episode with your cliffhanger (if applicable)?

6. Overall, are your scenes funny? They must be!

Dialogue Checklist

Have you taken an appropriate Pit Stop? You want to refuel your creativity before taking on the dialogue.

Exercise 56: With the checklist below, rewrite your dialogue.

1. Does the dialogue vary or sound like the same character?

Go through your script reading only one character's dialogue at a time. Highlight the main characters and their dialogue, using different colors. This helps illuminate inconsistencies in the character's dialogue and speech patterns. Repeat this process with each character in your script, checking each line:

   (a) Is it consistent for your character compass traits and dipstick?

   (b) Is it consistent with the character's relationship to whomever he/she is speaking?

   (c) Is it appropriate for the series and/or network?

Now, continue to examine the dialogue as a whole:

2. Do you need to jazz up your dialogue in the scene by using some of the dialogue devices discussed in Chapter Seventeen?

3. Does each line of dialogue fulfill at least one of the dialogue signposts listed in Chapter Seventeen?

4. Are you arriving late and leaving early in your dialogue in each scene?

Go through the dialogue within each scene and find the one line which is the fuel (essence) of that scene. Circle it. Then go back through the scene and toss as many unneeded lines before and after that line as you can. This is the time to look for repeating lines that don't need to be repeated.

For example: "I can't believe you did that. What were you thinking?"

You don't need both of these lines, one does the job. Remember, if it is the style of the series dialogue to often repeat lines, then that's okay. Follow the rules of the series.

Are we there yet? Are we there yet? Are we there yet? Almost.

Joke Checklist

After at least a one week Pit Stop, then:

Exercise 57: Follow the checklist for your jokes.

1. Do you have at least 2–3 jokes per page?

2. Is your setup subtle, or will the audience see it coming?

3. Is your setup succinct and relatable to the audience?

4. Have you created enough tension in the setup to be released in the punch line?

5. Is your punch line hysterical?!

6. Do you have variety in your jokes, or are they all comebacks or monologues? Remember, mix it up.

7. Are your jokes deriving naturally from the characters and the scene? Don't force the joke. The humor in your dialogue must flow effortlessly.

8. Have you exaggerated the comedy to the nth degree, both in visual/ sight gags and dialogue jokes? The bigger the better!

9. Did you go past the joke? If so, add a beat so the actor won't trample the next line of dialogue.

10. Are your jokes economical? Make sure they aren't too verbose, weighing down the laughs.

Prose Checklist

Hooray! It's time for that last polish.

Exercise 58: Follow the checklist for your prose.

1. Are you choosing action verbs and other strong word choices?

2. Have you eliminated all excess words?

3. Have you captured the sitcom's tone in your prose?

4. Have you capitalized all prose and underlined any movement by the actors, including entering and exiting?

Road Rule #26: Your first five pages must read brilliantly and be funny!

Exercise 59: After a Pit Stop of a few days, polish your first five pages again to ensure they are an exceptional read!

You did it! You survived the rewrite process. Be proud of your hard work, your script reflects all your efforts. Hopefully, it will pay off—literally.

Everybody's a Critic

This is fortunate for you because it's time to hand your scripts out to trusted friends to read. Choose friends who are brave enough to tell you what's funny and what isn't in your script. After you get their notes, take another Pit Stop (at least a week, preferably two weeks) to absorb the notes before polishing your script for the final time. The more time away from your script, the more objectively you can approach your polish. You might not use all the notes you get, but if you consistently get the same note on a certain area of your script, odds are, your friends are right.

Exercise 60: Polish your script regarding the comments you received, then set your first script aside and take another long Pit Stop. You've earned it. Go out and celebrate.

Exercise 61: Once you've refueled your creativity, then begin the process again. Go back through this book and complete the necessary writing exercises for your second script. Once you have completed your second half-hour script, its rewrite, and its polish, then you'll be ready to proceed to the next chapter.

Give yourself a round of applause. You've put in some very hard work. The time has come to send your scripts out into the world.

Chapter Twenty-one
Sitcoms or Bust!

Now that you've written, rewritten, and polished your scripts repeatedly until both read brilliantly, it's time to send them out. First, you'll have to send a query letter or make a cold call to get permission to submit your script to a series producer, and/or agent.

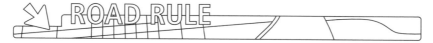

Road Rule #27: Never send your script to a producer or an agent without first getting permission!

How do you get permission? By contacting agents and producers. You can get names of producers and studio executives from The Hollywood Creative Directory of Producers and The Hollywood Creative Directory of Agents. The directories list who works where and what their title is, the studio/producer's (or agents) office address, phone number, and what films and/or television series they have produced. It's a handy book to have for a writer without an agent, but each costs about eighty dollars. You can purchase both books from Samuel French bookstore in Hollywood. In addition, there's a list of agencies and their addresses/phone numbers (without specific names of agents) that the Writer's Guild of America will send you for only a couple of dollars. The WGA Journal also periodically runs listings of each television series currently on air and contact information so it might be a good idea to check for that periodical at your local library.

In addition, here's a list of helpful writer stores which carry the above materials and script samples:

Larry Edmund Bookstores: (213) 463-3273
Samuel French Bookstore: (213) 876-0570
B. Dalton: (213) 469-8191

The Query Letter

This is a letter in which you make your request for submission. If you have written an original pilot script, you most definitely want to get an agent before you pitch your series anywhere. You need an agent to protect your interests. For those who have written two sample scripts of existing shows, I would also recommend finding an agent. Let them send your scripts out, but you can also try to pitch to series' producers. In your query letter, include as succinctly as possible:

1. That you have two half-hour scripts you would like the agent or producer to read. If speaking/writing to a series producer, let them know you are a devoted fan of the show and would like to pitch to them, after of course, they review your sample scripts. If you are speaking/writing to an agent, let them know that you are a writer seeking representation.

2. List any previous writing positions, credits, awards, and/or nominations you have acquired (even if it's not in the TV medium). You want to prove you are marketable as a writer.

3. Thank the person for his/her time for considering reading your script.

4. Just send the query letter, do not send your script until invited to do so by the producer or agent.

It's okay to send out multiple query letters. Hopefully, you'll receive positive responses, although it might be several weeks or even a month before you receive a reply. If you live in the Los Angeles area, make some cold calls. Introduce yourself to the assistant and briefly list any credits you have as a writer. Tell them you have a script you'd like to send. Be especially nice to these assistants as these are the people who will read your scripts first, and help you get your foot into the door. Be respectful of their time.

Exercise 62: Send out query letters or make cold calls to get your scripts read. Repeat this exercise until you have someone reading your script.

Keep a list of whom and when you sent letters or made calls to.

The Script Submission

You've finally received permission to submit your script, sent it off, and now it's being read by an assistant. These assistants are trusted by the agent or producer to find the next "hot" writer. They are your next speed bump in the road. If they like your scripts, then they will pass it on to the agent or producer for whom they work.

You will be judged on story structure, characters, dialogue, style, and humor (if applicable). If you haven't received a response three weeks after sending your scripts, then call. Don't pester, but be persistent. These people are extremely busy, and might have forgotten your script.

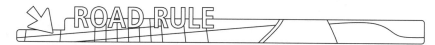

Road Rule #28: Don't take rejection personally!

There are too many factors that determine why someone passes on your script—besides your talent or the quality of your scripts. Don't be shy (but don't be defensive) when rejected. Ask for an honest critique of the script. Thank the reader for his/her time. If your script is rejected, send it to the next agent on the list, and keep sending until you find an agent who says yes. If a producer doesn't like your scripts, then he/she won't call you in to pitch for the series.

NOTE: If you receive enough feedback listing the same problems, then rewrite and polish that script before sending it out again. Wait until you have several of the same negative comments, however, because you don't want to tailor your script to someone who's already rejected it.

Let's say your scripts are received enthusiastically because you've followed the Writer's Road Map #5: Writing Sitcoms in a creative and successful way, proving your talents as a writer. Then zoom onto the express lane. You're on your way!

The Pitch

If a producer likes your scripts, then you will get a meeting to pitch your story ideas in hopes of landing a freelance assignment (and eventually a staff job). If an agent likes your original pilot, then you will pitch your series around town. For your story pitch, follow the story signposts, giving the beginning, middle, and end of your story. If it is an ensemble cast, create story ideas for several different characters. That way, if they have several Robert Barone *(Everybody Loves Raymond)* stories for example, then you could quickly start pitching a story for Marie or Debra. When pitching your series idea, follow the series signposts and capture the flair of the studio's style to which you are pitching.

Exercise 63: Using all story road flags, write your pitch for your each story idea or your series idea. Give the pitch flair. Then practice pitching it aloud just as you would pitch it in the meeting to producers. You can leave the written pitch behind with producers when you leave the meeting.

In your written pitch, include a title page with your name, and a 1–2 page summary of the series. List and describe who the major characters will be, the style of comedy, and what the series would be like from week to week. Include a few sample springboards or premises. Be as clever as you can.

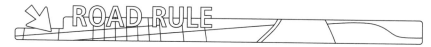

Road Rule #29: When you pitch, whether verbally or written, do so with enthusiasm! You are the one selling your screenplay. Don't be a doormat. Wow them!

In Conclusion

Get your scripts out there; get them read. Establish a network of contacts, because more than talent and more than luck, it's who you know! Build and keep relationships with Hollywood assistants, producers, executives, and agents. Your career depends upon it. You never know, someone's assistant today, may be running the studio tomorrow. Befriend everyone!

Each studio has its own signature style. Find the one that matches your own talents as a writer. Your career is what you make it. There will be bumps along the way, but if you have the endurance to stick with it, and follow *Gardner's Guide to TV Sitcom Writing: The Writer's Road Map*, you too, can have a very, very lucrative career. Good luck!

Sitcom Glossary

act-out line: the last line of character dialogue before the commercial break.

alliteration: a repetition of initial sounds in adjacent words or syllables.

antagonist: the villain or character who opposes the driver (hero).

A-story: the main plot of your episode.

B-story, C-story, D-story...: the subsequent subplots of your episode.

backstory: all the information about your character and his/her relationships to other characters that takes place before your episode and/or series begins.

b.g.: is used in scripts to abbreviate "background."

beat: a comedic or dramatic moment in a scene or a dramatic or comedic pause in dialogue.

blue humor: risqué humor or jokes about sex.

breaking the fourth wall: when a character turns and speaks directly into the camera or to the audience.

broad comedy: comedy that includes slapstick and farce.

callback joke: a joke that refers back only once to a previous joke in the episode that's already been setup and paid off.

central idea: the idea which sums up in one or two sentences who and what your story and/or series is about.

central (?) avenue: the question that spins the episode, story arc, and/or series. In your episode, this question is answered in the climax of Act Two.

cerebral comedy: comedy that shoots for the intellect by using brainy humor and witty repartee. Characters are educated, witty, and clever.

character arc: the learning curve (arc) of a character; i.e., what a character learns in the course of the episode, story arc, and/or series.

character compass: the major and minor character traits which establish a character's personality. It includes positive as well as negative traits.

character dipstick: a list of important moments in a character's life, and how they shaped his/her personality. It also includes any important relationship which shapes/has shaped the character, his/her backstory, and his/her physical traits.

character tag: the unique and fun description of a character. Used only when introducing a new character.

character tic: a trait or distinction given only to that particular character.

character trinity: the three major character elements which affect your plot: a character's goal, need, and fear.

city block: a story sequence composed of ten streets (scenes). It has its own beginning, middle, and end with obstacles and/or dilemmas which confront the drivers of the episode.

cliché: phrases which we have heard so often they become trite.

cliffhanger: a scene in which the driver is figuratively (and sometimes literally) hurled off a cliff and left hanging until next week's episode. This plot device teases viewers into tuning in the following week to find out what happens to the driver.

climax: the dramatic crash or confrontation for the driver which occurs at the end of the episode in Act Two.

cold calls: networking; making phone calls to development people, studio executives, and producers in order to introduce yourself and request permission to submit a sample script to them.

comeback: a sarcastic or humorous response by one character to another, sometimes known as a one-liner.

comedic catalysts and complications: popular ideas from which to spin and complicate sitcom stories.

comedy cones: mechanisms of humor that signal jokes and gags. They are devices which make your script wittier.

continuing central (?) avenue: a central question that continues throughout several episodes and/or the series; generally a romance subplot.

dialogue block: the lines of dialogue that make up a character's speech block.

dialogue devices: writer's tools used to jazz up dialogue, making it more interesting.

dialogue signposts: the questions used to measure whether or not you need a specific line of dialogue.

dissolve: to fade two adjacent scenes together, overlapping one image onto the other. This is used mostly to denote a passage of time.

driver: the protagonist or lead character of your story.

end tag: this is the resolution to the story summed up in a funny one minute clip that runs with or without the credits. It completes the story and gives the last joke of the episode.

episode arc: the story that peaks and then is concluded within an episode.

Est. shot: establishing shot; this is sometimes used to set up a location.

exposition: information needed by the viewer to understand the story or a character's motivations.

EXT.: exterior; describes the location in the slugline and is always abbreviated in capital letters.

falling rocks: the obstacles hurled at your driver during the episode, story, and/or series.

farce: comedy based on ludicrously improbable events and extremely ridiculous situations. It is absurd in its tone.

flashback: a scene which flashes back in time; a technique often used to give exposition.

flashfoward: a scene which flashes forward in time; a technique used most often for humor.

graphing: to outline scene by scene a television episode or script, listing the essence of each scene, who is in the scene, where and when the scene takes place, and what time the scene falls in the episode (by minutes) or script (by page).

green light: 10th Street; the scene at the end of Act One where the driver (hero) must commit to the story. The character speeds into the action full speed ahead.

hero: the driver of your story, your story's protagonist. This is the character the viewer roots for throughout your story.

high-concept: a series idea which can be conveyed in one or two sentences with a hook that makes the story easily recognized as becoming a successful and profitable series.

hook: a twist that makes the story idea fresh and original or turns it in a surprising manner.

INT.: interior; describes the location in the slugline; always abbreviated in capital letters.

intercut.: to cut quickly back and fourth between two scenes; most often used when two characters are talking via the telephone and the editor cuts back and forth to each character's location.

juxtapose: to place side by side for comparison.

monologue: a long block of dialogue belonging to one character, for example a speech, toast, eulogy, tirade, etc.…

music montage: a series of scenes without dialogue where music plays over the images. Often used to illustrate time passing, characters falling in love, reflect a tone or mood, or just for humor.

oblique scene: to write a scene that is unexpected, surprising the viewer and/or the character(s) in the scene and making the viewer laugh.

original run: the first time an episode airs on television.

one-two payoff: a gag that incorporates an action-reaction, and then an unexpected action. This technique builds tension because it creates a subconscious suspicion with the viewer which the sitcom writer can play for humor. You can play the one-two as many times as you like as long as it is followed by the payoff (punch line)

parallel plot: a subplot which mimics the main plot, telling basically same story, but through another character's POV.

parallel street: a subplot.

parody: a comical or satirical imitation of someone or something.

pilot script: the first script; that which creates the series and its characters.

pitch: to tell a story idea to executives/producers as succinctly and enthusiastically as possible.

pit stop principle: taking several days or several weeks off to refuel your imagination and gain perspective so you come back to your script with fresh energy.

plot: the structure of your story, the storyline.

point-of-view: (POV) from whose perspective the story is told.

pratfalls: physical trips, stumbles, and falls that an actor performs to get a laugh. They are physical sight gags.

props: items within the scene that the actor's touch or move about. For example, a glass, a gun, a pillow....

prose: the description or action in the scene; i.e. everything on the script page that isn't a slugline, dialogue block, or character names in caps.

protagonist: the main character of the story, the driver, the hero.

pun: the humorous use of a word in a way that suggests two or more interpretations.

punch line: the surprise or twist that completes the joke and gets the laugh.

put-down: name-calling and/or a type of insult.

query letter: a letter sent to acquire permission to submit a script. It should include the point of the letter, information about the writer, a brief synopsis of the sample script, and/or original series idea, and any acclaim the script has garnered.

residuals: the residual money paid to a writer every time an episode airs on television. The amount decreases incrementally with each airing to a set WGA standard percentage.

resolution: the conclusion or result of the storyline.

rest area: a scene in which the character and/or viewers can take a moment to rest from the tension of the plot. It serves as an emotional moment, character reveal, or comic relief.

road map: the writer's outline.

rule of three: playing a joke or gag three times, or repeating it for three times since three is the magic number in comedy.

runners: a storyline which runs through the series. Most often runners involve the romantic plot line of a series.

running gags: a gag which runs through the entire episode, story arc, or series.

running jokes: a joke which runs through the entire episode, story arc, or series. Characters may repeat the original joke, vary the joke, or add a new punch line. The difference between a callback joke and a running joke is that running jokes repeat more than once.

sample script: a script written to illustrate your work as a writer; used in hopes of getting freelance assignments based on the quality of the script. It is not a script written to be sold.

satirical comedy: a style of comedy that uses irony, ridicule, and sarcasm to expose folly or vice. It often contains cynical and humorous criticisms. Characters mock, tease, or spoof other characters. The humor is often irreverent and flippant.

scene: (street) a story unit. A scene changes any time the story moves to a new location or new time.

screen narration: information given to the audience via a character speaking to the viewer while the character is off screen, or narration written visually on the screen.

series arc: the peak and conclusion of the main continuing story in a series.

setup: introduces the subject of the joke in a succinct manner, and sets up the punch line.

setup, then payoff: this is a gag which is setup in the beginning of the episode, then is paid off sometime before the end of the episode.

signature line: a line of dialogue that a viewer identifies with only one certain character.

signposts: questions which check your dialogue, prose, jokes, etc.

sitcom premise: see springboards.

sitcom tunnel: the genre of the sitcom; family, friends, workplace, or combo with a lead star.

sitcom writing fines: errors created by writers that mark them as amateurs.

slapstick: numerous physical sight gags, in other words a lot of pratfalls and exaggerated mannerisms—think *Three's Company*.

slugline: the line which introduces each scene. It is always written in capital letters and underlined. It includes: whether the scene is exterior or interior, its location, and the time of day. For example:

INT. WILL'S APARTMENT—DAY or
EXT. CENTRAL PARK—DUSK.

spec script: a script written on the speculation that it will sell; for example, writing a pilot for an original series, then attempting to sell that script.

springboard: a sitcom premise that includes the central idea and the plot twist or hook of the A-story. It can also include a strong B-story, C-story, if the cast is truly ensemble; thus, any character can be the lead character in any given week. It sums up the beginning, middle, and end of the A-story in a succinct and witty way. It's the 3–6 pitch, whether written or verbal, to executives and producers.

story arc: the peak and resolution of the storyline. This may occur over the course of several episodes.

story incline: rising jeopardy for the characters in the plot.

story signposts: plot points which must be addressed on 10th and 11th Streets to increase dramatic tension in the story structure.

story speed limit: tension or suspense created in the plot.

street: a street equals one scene/beat or a series of very short scenes.

synopsis: a brief summary of a story.

teaser: the opening scene of an episode which encompasses the first several minutes, and entices the viewer into watching the rest of the episode.

teleplay: a script written for television.

ticking clock: a story device which sets up tension and a need for immediate action by the character. It dictates that a character will perform a certain action by a specific time, or a grave consequence will occur. Often this device is set into motion by the story's antagonist.

toppers: a joke which tops a punch line that's already been setup and paid off. It's an additional punch line to the first joke.

tow-away street: the story's catalyst, the scene/beat in Act One (or the Teaser) in which the driver is towed or pulled into the story.

triples: this is a joke that has two setups, then the punch line. Remember the magic rule of three?

try-fails: in this comedy cone, the character tries and fails, try and fails, over and over, either throughout the episode or the series.

two-part episode: a story which is told and concluded in two episodes instead of the usual half-hour format. In a two-part episode, generally the second half hour of the story is shown the following week, but it can air back-to-back on the same night.

ultimatum: a verbal order which implies a dire consequence if the order is not followed.

universal appeal: those emotional needs which we all have that hook viewers and cause them to care about the characters and what happens to them in the course of the story.

u-turn: 11th Street, the midpoint of the episode; the scene which turns the story in a totally new and unexpected direction.

voice over: (VO) is used when a character's voice is heard, but the character is not seen on the screen, or is not seen onscreen speaking the words being heard.

Sitcomography

In television, the producers are the writers, so below is a list of producing/writing credits. Executive producers are the head writers of a series. Sometimes there's an "&" listed and other times the word "and" listed. The "&" means a partnership whereas the word "and" infers that additional writers or producers worked on the series, but not as an exclusive partnership.

3rd Rock From The Sun: created by Bonnie Turner; executive producers Bill Martin, Bonnie Turner, Caryn Mandabach, Christian Zander, Marcy Carsey, Mike Schiff, Terry Turner, Tom Werner; co-executive producers Mark Brazill, Patrick Kienlen. NBC.

According to Jim: created by Joanthan Stark & Tracy Newman; executive producers Jonathan Stark, Mark Gurvitz, Suzanne Bukinik, Tracy Newman; staff writer Brent Piaskoski. ABC.
"Turkey Bowl" written by Tracy Gamble; directed by Gil Junger.

Alf: created by Paul Fusco & Tom Patchett; executive producer: Tom Patchett & Bernie Brillstein; producers: Paul Fusco. NBC.

Becker: creator Dave Hackel; executive producer Dave Hackel, Ian Gurvitz; co-executive producer Russ Woody; producer Matthew Weiner; co-producer Matthew Weiner; executive story editor Matthew Weiner. CBS.
"Cyrano DeBeckerac" written by Marsha Myers.
"The Usual Suspects" written by Ken Levine.

The Bernie Mac Show: creator Larry Wilmore; executive producer Larry Wilmore; producer Bernie Mac, Kellita Smith, Ken Kwapis, Marc Abrams, Michael Petok, Steve Greener, Teri Schaffer; co-executive producer Warren Hutcherson. FOX.

Bewitched: created by Sol Saks; executive producerHarry Ackerman; producer Danny Arnold, Jerry Davis; associate producer Ernie Losso, Jerry Briskin, Richard Michaels; executive consultant William Asher. ABC.

Black Adder Series: created by Richard Curtis and Rowan Atkinson
"A Black Adder's Christmas Carol" written by Richard Curtis and Rowan Atkinson. BBC.

The Bob Newhart Show: created by David Davis, Lorenzo Music; executive producer David Davis, George Zaloom, Jay Tarse, Les Mayfield, Lorenzo Music, Michael Zinberg, Tom Patchett; producer Bill Idelson, David Davis, Glen Charles, Jean-Michel Michenaud, Les Charles, Lorenzo Music, Martin Cohan; co-producer Charles Duncombe Jr. CBS.

Bosom Buddies: created by created by Chris Thompson; writers: Chris Thompson, Joel Zwick, David Chambers, Leonard Ripps, Roger Garrett, Will MacKenzie,

Jack Carrerow & David Chambers, David Lerner & Bruce Ferber. ABC.

The Brady Bunch: created by Sherwood Schwartz; executive producer Sherwood Schwartz; producer Howard Leeds II, Lloyd J. Schwartz; writers Arnold Peyser, Lois Peyser, Martin Ragaway, Larry Rhine, Tam Spiva, Skip Webster, Harry Winkler. ABC.

Cheers: created by creator Glen Charles, James Burrows, Les Charles; executive producer Bill Steinkellner, Cheri Steinkellner, Dan O'Shannon, Glen Charles, James Burrows, Les Charles, Peter Casey, Phoef Sutton, Tom Anderson; co-executive producer Dan Staley, Rob Long, producer David Angell, David Lee, Heide Perlman, Ken Estin, Peter Casey, Sam Simon; co-producer Andy Ackerman, Brian Pollack, David Isaacs, Ken Levine, Larry Balmagia, Mert Rich, Tom Leopold; executive story editor Kathy Ann Stumpe; story editor Fred Graver, Janet Leahy, Jeff Abugov, Rebecca Parr, Sue Herring. NBC.

The Cosby Show: created by Bill Cosby, Ed Weinberger, Michael Leeson; executive producer Bernie Kukoff, Bill Cosby, Caryn Mandabach, Janet Leahy, Marcy Carsey, Nancy Stern, Tom Werner; producer Adriana Trigiani, Carmen Finestra, Gary Kott, Gordon Gartrelle, John Markus, Matt Williams, Steve Kline, Terri Guarnieri. NBC.
"The Juicer" written by Matt Williams

Curb Your Enthusiasm: created by Larry David; executive producer Gavin Polone, Jeff Garlin, Robert B. Weide. HBO.
"The Benadryl Brownie" written by Larry David

"Club Soda and Salt" written by Larry David
"The Nanny" written by Larry David

Designing Women: created by Linda Bloodworth-Thomason; executive producer Harry Thomason & Linda Bloodworth-Thomason, Norma Stafford Vela. CBS.
"Big Haas and Little Falsie" written by Linda Bloodworth-Thomason.
"Foreign Affairs" written by Cheryl Bascam.
"Grand Slam, Thank You, Ma'am" written by Linda Bloodworth-Thomason.
"The Slumber Party" written by Linda Bloodworth-Thomason.

The Drew Carey Show: created by Bruce Helford, Drew Carey; executive producer Bruce Helford, Bruce Rasmussen, Clay Graham, Daniel O'Keefe, Dave Caplan, Deborah Oppenheimer, Drew Carey, Holly Hester, Les Firestein, Mike Teverbaugh, Richard Day, Robert Borden; Producer Bob Nickman, Brian Scully, Holly Sawyer, Jana Hunter, Larina Adamson, Lona Williams, Louis Fusaro, Mitch Hunter, Richard Baker, Rick Messina, Robert Borden, Terry Mulroy. ABC.
"Drew and the Activist II" written by Christy Jacobs White
"Golden Boy" written by Bruce Rasmussen.

Everybody Loves Raymond: created by Philip Rosenthal, executive producer David Letterman, Ray Romano, co-executive producer Cindy Chupack, producer Philip Rosenthal, executive story editor Steve Skvoran, Tucker Cawley; story editor Tom Caltabiano. CBS.

"Allie's Birth" written by Tucker Cawley.

"The Canister" written by David Regal.

"The Checkbook" written by John Fortenberry.

"Dancing With Debra" written by Aaron Shure & Steve Skrovan.

"Italy, Part 1" written by Philip Rosenthal.

"Italy, Part 2" written by Philip Rosenthal.

"The Lucky Suit" written by Tucker Cawley.

"Marie's Meatballs" written by Tucker Cawley.

"Marie's Sculpture" written by Jennifer Crittenden.

"Raybert" written by Steve Skrovan.

"Traffic School" written by Kathy Ann Stumpe.

"A Vote for Debra" written by Lew Schneider & Steve Skrovan.

"What Good Are You" written by Jennifer Crittenden.

Fawlty Towers: created by John Cleese & Connie Booth. BBC.

"Basil the Rat" written by John Cleese & Connie Booth.

"Gourmet Night" written by John Cleese & Connie Booth.

"The Kippers and the Corpse" written by John Cleese & Connie Booth.

Frasier: created by David Angell & David Lee & Peter Casey; executive producers Chris Marcil, Christopher Lloyd (II), Dan O'Shannon, David Angell, David Lee, Joe Keenan, Jon Sherman, Kelsey Grammar, Lori Kirkland, Mark Reisman, Peter Casey, Rob Hanning, Sam Johnson; producers Bob Daily, Eric Zicklin, Gayle Abrams, Maggie Blanc, Maggie Randell, Rob Greenberg, Saladin K. Patterson, Suzanne Martin, William Lucas Walker. NBC.

"Ain't Nobody's Business If I Do" written by Jay Kogen.

"An Affair To Forget" written by Chuck Ranberg & Anne Flett-Giordano.

"Call Me Irresponsible" written by Anne Flett-Giordano & Chuck Ranberg.

"Big Crane On Campus" written by Mark Reisman.

"Dial M for Martin" written by Rob Greenberg.

"The Flour Child" written by Chrisopher Lloyd II.

"The Focus Group" written by Rob Greenberg.

"Gift Horse" written by Ron Darian.

"Give Him The Chair" written by Chuck Ranberg & Anne Flett-Giordano.

"Here's Looking At You" written by Brad Hall.

"Kisses Sweeter Than Wine" written by Anne Flett-Giordano.

"Liar, Liar" written by Chuck Ranberg & Anne Flett-Giordano.

"A Lilith Thanksgiving" written by Chuck Ranberg & Anne Flett-Giordanod.

"Miracle on 3rd or 4th Street" written by Christopher Lloyd II.

"Moon Dance" written by Joe Keenan & Christopher Lloyd II & Rob Greenberg & Jack Burditt and Chuck Ranberg & Anne Flett-Giordano & Linda Morris & Vic Rauseo.

"Retirement Is Murder" written by Elias Davis & David Pollock.

"The Seal Who Came To Dinner" written by Joe Keenan.

"Someone To Watch Over Me" written by Don Seigel.

"Travels With Martin" written by Linda Morris & Vic Rauseo.

"The Two Mrs. Cranes" written by Joe Keenan.

The Fresh Prince of Bel Aire: created by Andy Borowitz & Susan Borowitz; executive producers Quincy Jones, Will Smith, Winifred Hervey; co-executive producer David Steven Simon; executive story editor Mike Soccio. NBC.
"Boyz in the Woods" written by Samm-Art Williams.

Friends: created by David Crane & Marta Kauffman; executive producer Adam Chase, David Crane, Greg Malins, Kevin S. Bright, Marta Kauffman, Michael Borkow, Michael Curtis; producer Alexa Junge, Betsy Borns, Ira Ungerleider, story editor Jeffrey Astroff, Mike Sikowitz, creative consultant Richard Rosenstock. NBC.
"The One On The Last Night" written by Scott Silveri.
"The One Where Joey Loses His Insurance" written by Andrew Reich & Ted Cohen. "The One Where Old Yeller Dies" written by Greg Malins & Adam Chase.
"The One With All The Resolutions" written by Suzie Villandry.
"The One With Chandler In A Box" written by Michael Borkow.
"The One With Mac and C.H.E.E.S.E." written by Doty Abrams.
"The One With Ross's Wedding, Part 2" written by Shana Goldberg-Meehan & Scott Silveri; story by Shelley Condon & Amy Toomin.
"The One With Russ" written by Ira Ungerleider.
"The One With The Thanksgiving Flashbacks" written by Greg Malins.

Full House: Jeff Franklin I, Robert L. Boyett, Thomas Miller; executive producer Jeff Franklin I, Robert L. Boyett, Thomas L. Miller; Bob Sagat; co-executive producer Ellen Guylas, Dennis Rinsler, Don Van Atta, Marc Warren III; producer Tom Amundsen, Greg Fields, Mark Fink, Bonnie Bogard Maier, James O'Keefe I, Dennis Rinsler, Leonard Ripps, David Steven Simon, Chuck Tatham, Jamie Tatham, co-producer Tom Burkhard, Boyd Hale, Kim Weiskopf. ABC.

The George Lopez Show: created by Bruce Helford, George Lopez, Robert Borden; executive producer Bruce Helford, Deborah Oppenheimer, Robert Borden, Sandra Bullock; co-executive producer Lawrence Broch; producer Brett Baer, Dave Finkel, George Lopez, Sandra Bullock;.co-producer Sandra Bullock. ABC.

Golden Girls: created by Susan Harris; executive producers Paul Junger Witt, Tony Thomas; producer Kathy Speer, Terry Grossman; co-producer Marsha Posner Williams. NBC.

Good Morning Miami: created by David Kohan, Max Mutchnick; executive producer David Kohan, Max Mutchnick; producer Tim Kaiser; consulting producer Jeanette Collins, Mimi Friedman; associate producer Bruce Alden. NBC.
"Jake's Nuts Roasting On An Open Fire" written by Kathy Ann Stumpe.

Happy Days: created by Edward Milkis, Garry Marshall, Thomas Miller; executive producer Edward Milkis, Garry Marshall, Thomas Miller; producer Lowell Ganz, Mark Rothman,

Nick Abdo, Tony Marshall; co-producer Ed Scharlach; creative consultant Milt Josefsberg. ABC.

Home Improvement: created by Carmen Finestra, David McFadzean, Matt Williams II; executive producer Tim Allen, Bob Bendetson, Bruce Ferber, Carmen Finestra, Matt Williams II, Gayle S. Maffeo, David McFadzean, Elliott Shoenman; co-executive producer Laurie Gelman, Maxine Lapiduss; producer Kim Tushinsky, Frank McKemy, Andy Cadiff, Howard J. Morris; co-producer Rosalind Moore, Jim Praytor. ABC.

I Dream of Jeannie: created by Sidney Sheldon; executive producer Sidney Sheldon; producer Claudio Guzmán, associate producer Sheldon Schrager, Joseph Goodson, Herb Wallerstein. NBC.

I Love Lucy: executive producer Desi Arnaz; producer Jess Oppenheimer I; head writer Bob Schiller; writers Bob Carroll Jr. I, Madelyn Pugh Martin, Bob Weiskopf. CBS

Just Shoot Me: creator by Steven Levitan; executive producer Bernie Brillstein, Brad Grey, David Guarascio, Jon Pollack, Kevin Slattery, Moses Port, Pamela Fryman, Steven Levitan;co-executive producer David Hemingson, David Walpert, John Peaslee, Judd Pillot; producer Allison Adler, Brett Baer, Bruce Rand Berman, David Finkel, Mike Lisbe, Nate Reger; co-producer Stephen Lloyd. NBC.
"How The Finch Stole Christmas" written by Stephen Engel.

"Lies and Dolls" written by Sivert Glarum.

Keeping Up Appearances: created by Roy Clarke I; executive producer and writer Roy Clarke I; produced by Harold Snoad. BBC.

King of the Hill: created by Greg Daniels & Mike Judge; executive producer Dave Krinsky, Glenn Berger, Howard Klein, John Altschuler, Jonathan Aibel, Michael Rotenberg, Mike Judge, Phil Roman, Richard Appel; co-executive producer Brent Forrester; producer Joseph A. Boucher; co-producer Daniel Rappaport, Glenn Berger, Joe Stillman, Jonathan Aibel; staff writer Garland Testa, Jim Dauterive, Johnny Hardwick, Norm Hiscock. FOX.

Mad About You: created by Danny Jacobson, Paul Reiser; executive producer Larry Charles, Danny Jacobson, Jeffrey Lane, Victor Levin; co-executive producer Victor Fresco, Sally Lapiduss, Barnet Kellman, Marjorie Weitzman; producer Bruce Chevillat, Robert Heath II, Helen Hunt, Steve Paymer, Paul Reiser. NBC.

Malcolm in the Middle: created by Linwood Boomer; executive producer Linwood Boomer; producer David Richardson; consulting producer Bob Kushell; story editor Alexandra Kaczenski, Dan Danko, Janae Bakken, John Bradford Goodman, Pang-Ni Landrum, Tom Mason. FOX.
"Baby, Part 1" written by Rob Hanning.
"Baby, Part 2" written by Michael Borkow.
"If Boys Were Girls" written by Nahnatchka Khan.
"Long Drive" written by Michael Borkow.

"Pilot" written by Linwood Bloomer.
"Watching the Baby" written by Rob Hanning.

Married With Children: creator Michael Moye & Ron Leavitt; executive producer Katherine Green, Kim Weiskopf, Michael Moye, Richard Gurman, Ron Leavitt; producer Barbara Blachut Cramer, Harriette Ames-Regan, Kevin Curran. FOX.

The Mary Tyler Moore Show: created by James L. Brooks & Allan Burns; executive producer James L. Brooks, Allan Burns; producer Stan Daniels, David Davis I, Ed. Weinberger; associate producer Budd Cherry. CBS.
"Chuckles Bites The Dust" written by David Lloyd.

M*A*S*H: developed for television by Larry Gelbat; based on the book M*A*S*H by Richard Hooker; executive producer Gene Reynolds, Larry Gelbart, Burt Metcalfe; producer Allan Katz I, Dennis Koenig, Jim Mulligan, Thad Mumford, John Rappaport, Don Reo, Dan Wilcox I. CBS.
"Abyssinia, Henry" written by Everett Greenbaum & Jim Fritzell.
"Adam's Ribs" written by Laurence Marks.
"Bananas, Crackers, and Nuts" written by Burt Styler.
"Change of Command" written by Everett Greenbaum & Jim Fritzell.
"Divided We Stand" written by Larry Gelbart.
"For Want of a Boot" written by Sheldon Keller.
"No Laughing Matter" written by Elias Davis & David Pollock.
"Sometimes You Hear The Bullet"

written by Carl Kleinschmitt.
"Tuttle" written by Bruce Shelley & David Ketchum.
"War of Nerves" written by Alan Alda.

Murphy Brown: creator Diane English; executive producer Bill Diamond, Candice Bergen, Gary Dontzig, Marc Flanagan, Michael Saltzman, Rob Bragin; co-executive producer David Sacks, Norm Gunzenhauser, Tom Seeley, Murphy Brown; producer Adam Belanoff, Bob Jeffords, Ned E. Davis; co-producer Jeffrey Ventimilia, Joshua Sternin,; executive story editor Bill Kunstler. CBS.
"Uh, Oh, Part 3" written by Korby Siamis & Diane English.

My Wife & Kids: creator Damon Wayans & Don Reo; executive producer Andy Cadiff, Damon Wayans, David Himelfarb, Don Reo, co-executive producer Eric Gold. ABC.
"Diary of a Mad Teen" written by Craig Wayans.
"Get Out" written by Dean Lorey.
"He Heard, She Heard" written by Buddy Johnson.
"A Little Romance" written by Don Reo & Damon Wayons.
"Road Trip" written by Rodney Barneg.

Newhart: developed by Sheldon Bull; creator Barry Kemp; executive producer Barry Kemp, Dan Wilcox, David Mirkin, Douglas Wyman, Mark Egan, Mark Solomon; co-executive Producer Bob Bendetson; producer Arnie Kogen, Barton Dean, Richard Rosenstock, Roy Teicher, Sheldon Bull; co-producer Michael Loman; executive story editor Gary Jacobs, Marshall Goldberg, Norm Gunzenhauser, Shelley Zellman, Tom

Seeley; story editor Barbara Hall, Bill Fuller, Billy Van Zandt, Dan O'Shannon, Ellen Herman, Jane Milmore, Jim Pond, Marjorie Gross, Michele Gendelman, Nell Scovell, Tom Anderson, Tom Seeley. CBS.
"The Last Newhart" written by Mark Egan & Mark Sobman & Bob Bendetson.

Reba: creator Allison M. Gibson; executive producer Allison M. Gibson, Kevin Abbott, Michael Hanel, Mindy Schultheis; co-executive producer Eric Horsted, Reba McEntire; producer Chris Alberghini, Jason Shubb, Mike Chessler; co-producer Lara Runnels, Patti Carr, Robert Peacock, Sabrina Wind. WB.

Sabrina, The Teenage Witch: creator Nell Scovell; executive producer Bruce Ferber, David Babcock, Paula Hart; co-executive producer Laurie Gelman; co-producer Dan Berendsen; producer Bruce Ferber, Frank Conniff, Kenneth R. Koch, Melissa Joan Hart; executive story editor Nick Bakay. ABC.

Saved By The Bell: created by Sam Bobrick; executive producer Peter Engel; producer Franco Bario, Sue Feyk; writer R.J. Colleary, Perry Dance, Brett Dewey, Mark Fink, David Garber II, Stephanie Garman.

Scrubs: creator Bill Lawrence; executive producer Bill Lawrence; consulting producer Matt Tarses; producer Bill Lawrence, Randall Winston; co-producer Gaby Allen, Garrett Donovan, Neil Goldman; story editor Mike Schwartz; staff writer Deb Fordham, Janae Bakken, Mark Stegemann. NBC.

"My First Day" (Pilot) written by Bill Lawrence.

Seinfeld: creator Jerry Seinfeld & Larry David; executive producer Alec Berg, Fred Barron, George Shapiro, Howard West, Jeff Schaffer, Jerry Seinfeld, Larry David; producer Carol Leifer, David Mandel, Marjorie Gross, Steve Koren; executive story editor Andy Robin, Gregg Kavet, Spike Feresten. NBC.
"The Busboy" written by Larry David & Jerry Seinfeld.
"The Contest" written by Larry David.
"The Good Samaritan" written by Peter Mehlman.
"The Limo" written by Larry Charles; story by Marc Jaffe.
"The Marine Biologist" written by Ron Hague & Charles Rubin.
"The Opera" written by Larry Charles.
"The Parking Garage" written by Larry David.
"The Puffy Shirt" written by Larry David.
"The Stall" written by Larry Charles.
"The Stranded" written by Larry David & Jerry Seinfeld and Matt Goldman.
"The Yada, Yada" written by Peter Mehlman and Jill Franklyn.

Sex & the City: created by Darren Star; executive producer Cindy Chupack, Darren Star, Michael Patrick King; co-executive producer Sarah Jessica Parker; creative consultant Julia Sweeney. HBO.
"All or Nothing" written by Jenny Bicks.
"The Caste System" written by Darren Star.
"My Motherboard, My Self" written by Julie Rottenberg & Elisa Zuritsky.
"The Perfect Present" written by Cindy Chupack.
"Unoriginal Sin" written by Cindy Chupack.

The Simpsons: created by developed by James L. Brooks, Matt Groening, Sam Simon; creator Matt Groening; executive producer Al Jean, Bill Oakley, David Mirkin, George Meyer, James L. Brooks, Josh Weinstein, Matt Groening, Mike Reiss, Mike Scully, Sam Simon; co-executive producer Richard Appel, Rob LaZebnik; producer Jon Vitti, Mike Scully, Richard Sakai; co-producer Paul Germain; story editor David X. Cohen; staff writer Conan O'Brien. FOX.

Sister, Sister: created by J. David Marks, Gabe Sumner; executive producer J. David Marks, Gabe Sumner; writers Ginny Cerrella, Joel Cohen I, Bill Condon; producer Pegi Brotman, Walter Coblenz.

South Park: created by Matt Stone, Trey Parker; executive producer Brian Graden, Deborah Liebling, Matt Stone, Trey Parker; producer Anne Garefino, David Niles White; story editor Paul Shomer; staff writer Kyle McCulloch, Matt Stone, Nancy Pimental, Trey Parker; creative consultant Pam Brady; writer Dan Sterling, David Goodman, Kyle McCulloch, M.C. Goldstein, Matt Stone, Nancy Pimental, Pam Brady, Philip Stark, Trey Parker, Trisha Nixon, Tupac Schwartz. COMEDY CHANNEL.

Spin City: creator Bill Lawrence & Gary David Goldberg; executive producer Andy Cadiff, Bill Lawrence, David S. Rosenthal, Jon Pollack, Michael J. Fox, Tom Hertz; producer Walter Barnett. ABC.

That 70's Show: created by Bonnie Turner, Linda Wallem, Mark Brazill, Terry Turner; executive producer Bonnie Turner, Caryn Mandabach, Jackie Filgo, Jeff Filgo, Jeffrey Ventimilia, Marcy Carsey, Mark Brazill, Terry Turner, Tom Werner; co-executive producer Joshua Sternin, Linda Wallem; producer Christine Zander, Franco Bario, Gregg Mettler, Joel Madison, Mark Hudis, Patrick Kienlen, Phillip Stark; co-producer Dean Batali, Jackie Behan, Linda Wallem, Rob des Hotel, Will Forte. FOX.
"Immigrant's Song" written by Rob Des Hotel.

Three's Company: created by Brian Cooke I, Johnnie Mortimer; executive producer Budd Grossman, Don Nicholl, Michael Ross XI, Bernard West; produced by John Baskin, George Burditt, Gene Perret, Bill Richmond II, Roger Shulman, Joseph Staretski, George Sunga; writer Martin Rips, Mark Tuttle I, Paul Wayne, Mike Weinberger, Kim Weiskopf, Shelley Zellman. ABC.

Will & Grace: created by David Kohan & Max Mutchnick; executive producer David Kohan, James Burrows, Jeff Greenstein, Max Mutchnick; co-executive producer Alex Herschlag, Jhoni Marchinko, Kari Lizer; producer Bruce Alden, Peter Chakos; co-producer Bill Wrubel. NBC.
"And The Horse He Rode In On…" written by Adam Barr.
"A Chorus Lie" written by Tracy Poust & Jon Kinnally.
"Crazy In Love" written by Tracy Poust & Jon Kinnally.
"Gypsies, Tramps, And Weed" written by Katie Palmer.
"It's The Gay Pumpkin, Charlie Brown" written by Gary Janetti.
"Leo Unwrapped" written by Sonja Warfield.
"The Needle And The Omelette's Done"

written by Tracy Poust & Jon Kinnally.
"Past and Presents" written by Tracy
Poust & Jon Kinnally.
"Sweet and Sour Charity" written by Gail
Lerner.

The Wonder Years: created by Neal Marlens
& Carol Black; executive producer Neal
Marlens & Carol Black; co-executive
producer Bob Brush, Jill Gordon;
producer Jeffrey Silver; Ken Topolsky,
Matthew Carlson, Michael Dinner,
David Chambers, Gina Goldman,
Denise Moss, Sy Dukane, Mark B. Perry,
Mark Levin. ABC.
"The Pimple" written by David M. Stern
& Todd W. Langen.
"The Tree House" written by Matthew
Carlson; story by Daniel M. Stern.

TV Sitcom Road Map

Series Title:	
Episode Title:	
A-Story Central Idea:	
B-Story Central Idea:	
C-Story Central Idea:	
D-Story Central Idea:	
Springboard:	
Character's Goal:	
Character's Need:	
Character Arc (if applicable):	

The Structure

Act One

1ST	*Tow-Away Zone or*
2ND	*Tow-Away Zone*
3RD	
4TH	
5TH	
6TH	
7TH	
8TH	
9TH	*Greenlight or*
10TH	*Greenlight*

Act Two

11TH	*U-Turn*
12TH	
13TH	
14TH	
15TH	
16TH	
17TH	
18TH	
19TH	
20TH	*Climax (and possible cliffhanger)*

End Tag — Resolution:

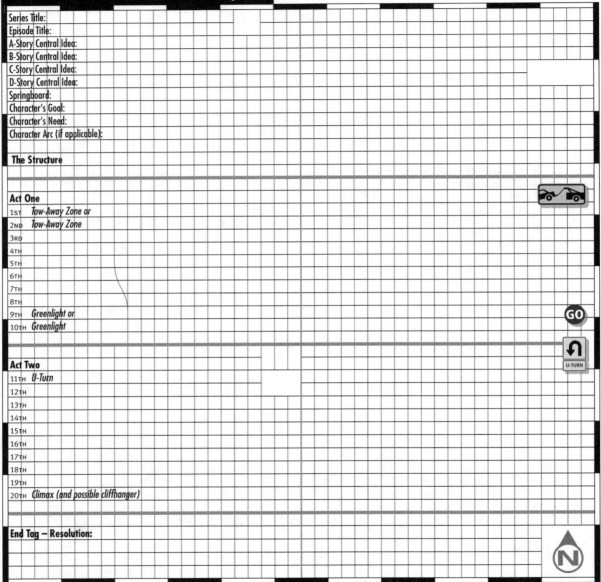

This map is designed to be enlarged on a photocopier at 130% on an 11" x 17" sheet

Index